Music in
Mainland Southeast Asia

Music in Mainland Southeast Asia

∞

EXPERIENCING MUSIC, EXPRESSING CULTURE

∞

GAVIN DOUGLAS

New York   Oxford
OXFORD UNIVERSITY PRESS
2010

Oxford University Press, Inc., publishes works that further Oxford University's objective of excellence in research, scholarship, and education.

Oxford   New York
Auckland   Cape Town   Dar es Salaam   Hong Kong   Karachi
Kuala Lumpur   Madrid   Melbourne   Mexico City   Nairobi
New Delhi   Shanghai   Taipei   Toronto

With offices in
Argentina   Austria   Brazil   Chile   Czech Republic   France   Greece
Guatemala   Hungary   Italy   Japan   Poland   Portugal   Singapore
South Korea   Switzerland   Thailand   Turkey   Ukraine   Vietnam

Published by Oxford University Press, Inc.
198 Madison Avenue, New York, New York 10016
http://www.oup.com

Library of Congress Cataloging-in-Publication Data

Douglas, Gavin, 1967–
Music in mainland Southeast Asia : experiencing music, expressing culture / Gavin Douglas.
   p. cm.—(Global music series)
Includes bibliographical references and index.
ISBN 978-0-19-536782-9 (pbk. (main))—ISBN 978-0-19-536783-6 (hardback)
1. Music—Southeast Asia—History and criticism.   2. Southeast Asia—Social life and customs.   I. Title.
ML330.D68   2009
780.959—dc22   2009022260

Printing number: 9 8 7 6 5 4 3 2 1

Printed in the United States of America
on acid-free paper

GLOBAL MUSIC SERIES

General Editors: Bonnie C. Wade and Patricia Shehan Campbell

Contents

Foreword

∝

In the past three decades interest in music around the world has surged, as evidenced in the proliferation of courses at the college level, the burgeoning "world music" market in the recording business, and the extent to which musical performance is evoked as a lure in the international tourist industry. This has encouraged an explosion in ethnomusicological research and publication including production of reference works and textbooks. The original model for the "world music" course—if this is Tuesday, this must be Japan—has grown old as has the format of textbooks for it, either a series of articles in single multi-authored volumes that subscribe to the idea of "a survey" and have created a canon of cultures for study, or single-authored studies purporting to cover world musics or ethnomusicology. The time has come for a change.

This Global Music Series offers a new paradigm. Instructors can now design their own courses; choosing from a set of case study volumes, they can decide which and how much music they will teach. The Series also does something else; rather than uniformly taking a large region and giving superficial examples from sev eral different countries within it, case studies offer two formats—some focused on a specific culture, some on a discrete geographical area. In either case, each volume offers greater depth than the usual survey. Themes significant in each instance guide the choice of music that is discussed. The contemporary musical situation is the point of departure in all the volumes, with historical information and traditions covered as they elucidate the present. In addition, a set of unifying topics such as gender, globalization, and authenticity occur throughout the series. These are addressed in the framing volume, *Thinking Musically* (Wade), which sets the stage for the case studies by introducing those topics and other ways to think about how people make music meaningful and useful in their lives. *Thinking Musically* also presents the basic elements of music as they are practiced in musical systems around the world so that authors of each case study do not have to spend time explaining them and can delve immediately into the particular music. A second framing volume, *Teaching Music*

Globally (Campbell), guides teachers in the use of *Thinking Musically* and the case studies.

The series subtitle, "Experiencing Music, Expressing Culture," also puts in the forefront the people who make music or in some other way experience it and also through it express shared culture. This resonance with global studies in such disciplines as history and anthropology, with their focus on processes and themes that permit cross-study, occasions the title of this Global Music Series.

Bonnie C. Wade
Patricia Shehan Campbell
General Editors

Preface

∽

The process of writing this book has reminded me of the extreme diversity and variety of traditions found in Mainland Southeast Asia. With hundreds of ethnicities, languages, and musical traditions found throughout the region it is clear that Mainland Southeast Asia is not one thing and studying it requires a diversity of perspectives.

In this book I hope to communicate several basic concepts that will provide not only a doorway into the musical worlds of the Southeast Asian peninsula but also will be useful to understanding music throughout the world. The book will provide an overview of several well-known traditions and some others that have received much less attention in scholarship and textbooks. It will guide you through some of the most beautiful sounds from the area but will also stress that music is not simply for enjoyment. Aesthetically engaging sounds are always socially contextualized and, as such, can teach us something about social, religious, political, or other types of identities.

As with other volumes in the Global Music Series, this book is guided by three themes that weave throughout the text. While specific chapters aim to focus attention on one theme over the others, the topics of diversity, political struggle and globalization are intimately intertwined in all chapters and cannot, ultimately, be separated. I chose these issues based on my travels in the area and on what I find other scholars today to be wresting with. The wide variety of ethnicities and languages throughout the countries in question demands some exploration into the role that music plays in asserting distinct cultural identities. All countries in the region have endured wars, uprisings, coups, etc., and the stories of these political struggles can be heard in the music. Lastly, the impact of globalization, a topic that appears in several other volumes of the global music series, is changing many of the musics and the musical behaviors throughout the region at a rapid pace.

Along with the traditions presented I hope I have conveyed a sufficient number of counter examples that break the mold and upset stereotypes of homogenous sounds and behaviors across the area. Traditions and identities are malleable: constantly changing to accommodate or challenge lived experiences. Mainland Southeast Asia is neither mono-lithic nor static. One manner by which I challenge this notion is through an attempt to bring many contemporary sounds into the discussion.

Given that this book traverses an area containing several language families and multiple distinct languages and dialects (I mention at least ten in the text), I have tried my best to convey terminology in the most user-friendly manner possible. In many cases there are multiple spellings for instruments and traditions in circulation. I have included numerous additional spellings of said terms in the glossary and, for the most part, have adopted the most frequently used spelling for the text.

ACKNOWLEDGMENTS

This book could not have been completed without an immense amount of assistance from a wide variety of people. My first thanks go to the hundreds of musicians that I listened to, played music with, and befriended throughout my fieldwork. Some are mentioned below, some appear in the text and many (particularly in Burma/Myanmar) cannot be named for reasons that will become apparent.

Special thanks go to Bonnie Wade and Patricia Shehan Campbell, the editors of the Global Music Series. Bonnie's tireless, close, and critical editing was extremely constructive and the book would look quite different (indeed would not exist) without her guiding hand and Pat's consistent encouragement helped through the tougher writing periods. Thanks to Cory Schneider and all the folks at Oxford for keeping me on task, reading closely, and for handling the voluminous press logistics. A big "thank you" to the reviewers of the manuscript, those that made themselves known to me and those that didn't: Lisa Gold, San Francisco Conservatory of Music; David Harnish, Bowling Green State University; Ellen Koskoff, Eastman School of Music, University of Rochester; Pamela A. Moro, Willamette University; Sean Williams, Evergreen State College; and, Deborah Wong, University of California, Riverside. I learned a great deal from your comments. Special thanks also to U Ko Ko, U Myint Maung, Ko Du, Terry Miller, Amy Catlin-Jairazbhoy, Robert Garifas, Pornprapit Phosavadi, Phong Nguyen, Rick Heizman, Laurel Sercombe and Andrea Emberly at The University of Washington Ethnomusicology Archives, The University of Montreal, Bob Haddad, Maung Maung Htwe, Gita Lulin U Ko Ko, William Southerland, Don Traut, Mark Engebretson, Adam Ricci, John Deal and the UNCG School of Music, and to my "Music of Southeast Asia" and "Modern Asia Through Its Music" classes that tested some of the early material. While

I could not have accomplished this project without the advice and assistance of all these people, all errors of fact and judgment are my own.

Finally, to my family: Jaiden and Nova, thanks for continually reminding me of my real priorities. All my love to Nadja for her faith, support, and patience throughout this project.

CD Track List

1. Musical offerings at Erawan shrine in Bangkok, Thailand. Recorded by Blutey in 1998. Permission given by Blutey.

2. Cambodian Flute Player, amputee flute player at Angkor Temple. Field recording by Gavin Douglas, 2003.

3. Nat Pwe, Spirit Propitiation Ceremony. Taungbyoan, Myanmar. Field recording by Gavin Douglas, 1998.

4. Parrita Chant, Theravada Buddhism. Field recording, Taunggyi, Myanmar. Field recording by Gavin Douglas, 1999.

5. Theravada Chant from monk initiation ceremony, "Three Gems", Field recording by Gavin Douglas 1999.

6. Burmese Saing Waing "Pabawin Tachin" Song by Sein Be Da with song text by Saya Tyin. Sung by Shwei Daung Myaing. Performed by the saing waing troupe of Shwei Daung Myaing (Golden Peacock) Field recording by Robert Garfias 1974.

7. Burmese Patt Waing, Sein Kyaw Naing, tuning field recording by Gavin Douglas, 1999.

8. Burmese Hne, solo. Hne U Mya Gyi. Field recording by Gavin Douglas, 1998.

9. Burmese Saung Gauk "In Praise of the Burmese Harp" *Mahagitá: Harp and Vocal Music of Burma.* U Myint Maung, Saung. Used by permission Smithsonian Folkways recordings SFW CD 40492. © 2003.

10. Burmese Pattala, solo "Myaman Giri" *Piano Birman/Burmese Piano: U Ko Ko.* UMMUS série traditions. UMM 203.

11. Thai Piphat ensemble "Sounds of the Surf Overture" ("Pleng Homrong Kleun Kratob Fang") *Royal Court Music of Thailand.* Used by permission Smithsonian Folkways Recordings. SF CD 40413. © 1994.

12. Khmer Pinn peat ensemble "Roeung Supheak Leak" *Echoes from the Palace: Court Music of Cambodia. Sam-Ang Sam Ensemble* Owl's Head Music CDT-140.

13. Thai Kruang Sai "Heart of the Sea," Used by permission Smithsonian Folkways Recordings. SF CD 40413. © 1994.

14. Vietnamese Dan Bau "Liêu Giang" (Liêu River), Phong Nguyen, *Vietnam: Mother Mountain and Father Sea*. White Cliffs Media WCM 9991.

15. Vietnamese Dan Tranh "Tam Nhac Dan Tranh" *Song of the Banyan: Folk Music of Vietnam*, Phong Nguyen ensemble. Owl's Head Music LAT 50607.

16. Cải Lương musical theater, Excerpt of Câu Thơ Yên Ngựa, A Poem on Horseback *Vietnam: Mother Mountain and Father Sea*. White Cliffs Media WCM 9991.

17. Pa-O procession, Taunggyi, Burma/Myanmar. Field recording by Gavin Douglas, 1998.

18. Shan ozi ensemble from Taunggyi, Burma/Myanmar. Field recording by Gavin Douglas, 1998.

19. Danu ozi ensemble from Taunggyi, Burma/Myanmar. Field recording by Gavin Douglas, 1998.

20. Karen Christmas Carolers, Rangoon, Burma/Myanmar. Field recording by Gavin Douglas, 1998.

21. Khaen and Morlam "Lam Tan Vey" *Bamboo Voices: Folk Music from Laos*. Khamvong Insixiengmai Ensemble. Owl's Head Music LAT50601.

22. Hmong Qeej, "New Year's song"(Qeej Kawm Ntawv) Produced by Alan Govenar, Courtesy Documentary Arts, Inc. *Boua Xou Mua: Music of the Hmong People of Laos*. Arhoolie CD 446.

23. Kong Nai, "Farewell Wishes" *Master Kong Nay & Ouch Savy: Mekong Delta Blues*. Real World Works Ltd. RWLT002.

24. Paritta Sutta: protection chantings, "Metta Sutta," Venerable Mingun Saydaw U Vicittasarabhivamsa, http://vipassanasangha. free.fr/=eng/paritta_sutta_by_sutta.htm

25. "Tantya teh shin" played on pattala. Demonstration by Gavin Douglas.

26. Burmese Piano, Yodaya thachin "Myanman Giri," *Piano Birman/ Burmese Piano: U Ko Ko*. UMMUS série traditions. UMM 203.

27. U Aung Shein, Guitar "Myaman Giri," Rangoon, Burma/Myanmar. Field recording by Gavin Douglas, 2005.

28. Banjo and Guitar, "Never on a Sunday," Rangoon, Burma/Myanmar. Field recording by Gavin Douglas, 2005.

29. Vietnamese Guitar, Kim Sinh "Li Giao Duyen," *The Art of Kim Sinh* 1992. World Music Library KICW 1061.

30. praCH, "Resurecc" *Dalama: The End'n' is Just the Beginnin*," 2000. http://www.mujestic.com/p__r__a__c__h

31. Future Burmese Generation "Let Us Be United," http://www.mmfg. netfirms.com/index2.html

CHAPTER 1

Diversity and Commonality

THREE VIGNETTES

Vignette 1: Erawan Shrine. I emerge from the skytrain at Chitlom station and a wave of heat, thick with moisture and rich with the smells of cooking grease and motor oil, hits me in the face. It's only 10:00 in the morning but the smells of Bangkok are unmistakable (Figure 1.1). Food kiosks line the sides of the streets that are choked with far more traffic than the city can handle—a consequence of Thailand's economic gains throughout the 1980s and 1990s. From the platform the street level is down several stories. At the intersection of Rachadamri and Phloenchit Roads I can see the behemoth Central Plaza Center (formerly called the World Trade Center) across the street, the Gaysorn Plaza and Amarin Plaza up the road, and the handicrafts store, Naraiphan, a favorite of Bangkok's many tourists. Opportunities to shop in huge air-conditioned malls are everywhere.

Passing dozens of street vendors selling trinkets, tee-shirts, food, and garlands, passing a McDonalds and a Japanese sushi restaurant, I come to San Phra Phrom or the Erawan Shrine (Figure 1.2). Connected to the Grand Hyatt Erawan Hotel, this shrine is placed right at the busy street intersection. Erected in 1956 for protection, Erawan shrine has a reputation for bringing good luck. For insurance on their way to and from work or on a break from shopping, devotees and tourists enter to donate flowers and incense and make wishes. If the requested wish is fulfilled, they will need to come back and pay the dancers/musicians to perform for the deity. The Phra Prom deity with shiny gold gilded on its four arms and four faces has clear Hindu origins yet comfortably finds a home in this predominantly Buddhist country. An ensemble of traditional Thai dancers and musicians playing drums and xylophones takes donations and makes musical and dance offerings to the deity (CD track 1).

Amidst this cosmopolitan hustle and bustle the Erawan Shrine offers a brief, almost peaceful, respite from the chaos outside the gates even as

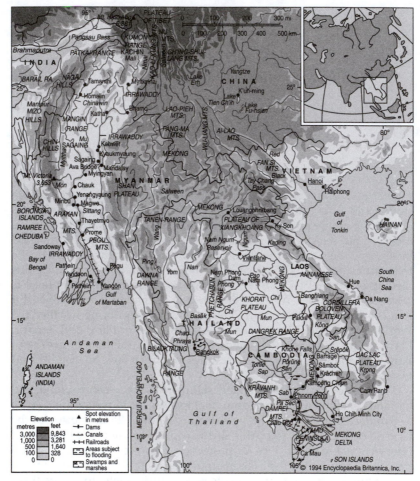

FIGURE 1.1　*Map of mainland Southeast Asia.*

the rumble of trains echoes from overhead. Modern space here encompasses traditional religious practice and musical engagement.

Vignette 2: Flute Player at Angkor Wat.　A year later I am back in Southeast Asia. I had heard a great deal of the famous ruins of Angkor, a series of temple complexes stretching through the Cambodian jungle for miles in every direction. This was the grand center of the Khmer

FIGURE 1.2   *Erawan Shrine, Bangkok. Dancers and Musicians can be seen in the background.   (Photo by Don Traut.)*

Empire (9th–15th centuries), one of the most powerful civilizations in Southeast Asia. At the height of its power the Khmer empire occupied much of present day Thailand to the west and stretched down into the Mekong delta of present day Vietnam in the southeast. Wandering through the stone passageways of the 12th century ruins of Angkor Thom—the last capital of the empire, which in its day would have rivaled the splendor of any major city in Europe—I hear an evocative melody played on a lone bamboo flute (CD track 2).

Slowly the melody developed from note to note with quick ornaments at the ends of each long plaintive phrase. I follow the sound around a corner of the maze surrounded by hundreds of images drawn from Hindu and Buddhist stories carved into the walls surrounding me. There before me is a legless man leaning against the wall. He stops playing, looks at me, smiles and waves me towards him (Figure 1.3). In broken English and French he shares his story of stepping on a landmine in the late 1970s during the devastating Khmer Rouge occupation (1975–79). Even today landmines from the Khmer Rouge and Vietnamese occupation eras continue to create amputees causing one of the highest rates of physical disability of any country in the world. While census data

FIGURE 1.3   *Disabled musician outside of Angkor Thom in the Angkor Wat area of Cambodia.*

for Cambodia is sketchy, it is generally accepted that more than 40,000 Cambodians have suffered amputations as a result of mine injuries since 1979. Twenty five years later this flute player rides each day on the back of his friend's bicycle to one of many spots around the Angkor Wat area to play for temple visitors, tourists primarily, who have traveled long distances to see this magnificent wonder of the ancient world.

With the normalization of Cambodia's economy and political system in the late 1990s, Cambodia has been able to slowly lure foreigners to its stunning historical artifacts and thereby provide greater opportunities for many of its people. As I meandered around the temple ruins for the next several days, I met multiple musicians performing at the gates of different temples. The majority of these musicians in the Angkor area (some formally trained, others not) are landmine victims. Music provided an opportunity to make a living playing for tourists and temple goers and to continue a tradition that was close to dying out.

Vignette 3: A Spirit Festival. Ten kilometers north of Mandalay (see Figure 1.1) is the village of Taungbyon, the epicenter of the cult of the *nat* spirits. *Nats* are animistic spirits that pre-date the Burmese adoption of Buddhism in the 11th century. The *nats* are regularly propitiated and consulted in regard to daily problems. Lack of attention to them can also cause problems in one's life. The *nat* cult is practiced in conjunction with Buddhism in Burma/Myanmar and large festivals designed to celebrate and consult with them are found throughout the country. I had traveled up from Yangon with a troupe of thirty musicians and actors to consecrate a statue of the great Buddhist abbot the Mingun Sayadaw U Vicittasarabivamsa. The abbot had died several years earlier but was remembered for his ability to memorize and recall the entire body of Buddhist texts (the *Tripitaka*) and was revered for his command of Buddhist philosophy. Despite his death the monk was still felt to be a spiritual guide for many Buddhists. While this troupe had traveled north to perform at the Mingun monastery (across the river from Mandalay) and to gain *kammic* (*karmic*) merit in the process, several musicians took this as an opportunity to visit a *nat* festival or *nat pwe* at Taungbyon. Practicing Buddhism and propitiating an animistic *nat* spirits seemed quite contradictory to me at the time. Not so to my hosts.

While it was only 9:00 in the morning we arrived at the Taungbyon shrine to a colorful, noisy, chaotic, party-like atmosphere. Here devotees of the spirit *nats* would trance dance to appease and, hopefully, win their favor. Though there are officially 37 *nats* in the pantheon, in practice there are many more. This shrine is dedicated to the Taungbyon brothers, twin brothers associated with the founding of the first Burmese kingdom founded in Pagan in the 11th century. They were erroneously killed by King Anawrahta (1044–1077) and, like other *nats* that are spirits of unjust or "green" deaths, have lingered over the past 900 years bestowing blessings and wreaking havoc on people.

While seemingly a contradiction and a clash to non-Burmese understandings of Buddhism (see Spiro 1996), to many Burmese the layering of animism and Buddhism is not a contradiction. Rather, the two complement each other. While Buddhism deals with the ultimate questions of existence (kammic law, Nirvana, enlightenment, etc.) and matters of universal concern, *nats* are spirits of this mundane world that can help or hinder daily life. They can bring wealth or sickness in the here and now. Devotees must propitiate the *nat* spirits with offerings of food, alcohol, money, and music. Next to the Taungbyoan brothers shrine is a large Buddhist *stupa*, a shrine built to hold a relic of the Buddha (a hair, a bone, a tooth fragment) or at least to remind people of the Buddha. The fact that these two spiritual/religious traditions exist literally side by side provides no conflict for devotees of the *nat* cult. While Myanmar is close to 90% Buddhist, a large number of these people actively participate in the *nat* cult. In recent years, with an oppressive government at the helm, *nat* worship has actually been on the rise as people attempt to come to terms with and find answers for the difficulty of their lives.

In front of the dancing area is an altar with images of the two brothers (Figure 1.4). Devotees and *nat kadaws* invite the *nats* to possess their bodies. *Nat kadaws* are wives of the *nats* who act as liaisons between

FIGURE 1.4 *Nat Shrine. The shrine of the Taungbyon nat brothers, in front of which devotees dance for the nat spirits.*

the spirits and visitors. They are often, but not exclusively, male trans-
vestites and constitute a unique gender category in Burma/Myanmar:
not masculine, not feminine, but a wife of the *nat* spirit. If readers are
interested in examining the flexible notions of transvestism and gender
within the *nat* spirite cult I recommend one of the few Burmese novels
translated into English, *Smile as they Bow*, by Nu Nu Yi.

To the far end of the venue is a *saing waing* troupe. The *saing waing*
ensemble is comprised of *patt waing* (drum circle of 21 tuned drums),
kyi waing (brass gong circle), *hne* (reed aerophone), and an assortment
of drums and gongs (see Chapter 2). It is the most important ensemble
in Burmese music with associations to the royal court and the country's
rich theatrical traditions. In this context, however, the *saing waing* troupe
is specially trained to play songs for the *nats* (CD track 3). The repertoire
of court and theatrical music has no place here, as specific compositions
will be played to invite specific *nats* to the event and to facilitate the
trance dance of the devotees and the *nat kadaws*. Dancers are dressed
in fabulously brilliant colors; they jump and spin in devotional ecstasy.
The ensemble plays through overdriven loudspeakers that distort melodies to unrecognizable fuzz. Dancers, now embodying the *nat* spirits,
consume excessive quantities of alcohol (mostly Johnnie Walker scotch)
and cigarettes, and the spirits are appeased.

Drawn from my experiences in Thailand, Cambodia and Burma/
Myanmar, these three vignettes provide contrasting perspectives of
musical life in mainland Southeast Asia. Each portrays the presence of
traditional music in a modern context. In each of these contexts the music
helps participants connect to traditional values and to a sense of cultural identity in the face of the quickly changing modernized world. In
the coming chapters, I will provide numerous other examples of people
musically defining their cultural identities in relation to other ethnicities, countries, and religions, as a way of asserting a political agenda or
recovering from war, or as a way of negotiating the forces of globalism.

ACTIVITY 1.1 *When you think about mainland Southeast
Asia, what images come to mind? Make an inventory of items,
images, and concepts that you have of this area of the world.
What cultural elements or issues come to mind? What political
images? Religious? Be as specific as you can as you jot these ideas
down on paper.*

> *Following from these broader generalizations, what conceptions do you have of Southeast Asian musics or sounds? Can you think of particular instrument types, timbres, or musical contexts?*
>
> *Finally, reflect on how these images and ideas have come to you. Are they based on first hand experience traveling in the area? Are they rooted in your relations with people from these communities? If not based on personal experience, then what type of media delivered them to you (international news, movies, travel accounts, friends, classes, etc.)?*
>
> *Listen to the first three tracks from the CD. In what ways do they conform or clash with your sonic preconceptions of mainland Southeast Asian music?*

For many readers in the West, the Southeast Asian peninsula will have been transmitted most forcefully through news media and pop culture as they report on the Vietnam War and its continuing legacy, genocidal atrocities in Cambodia, human rights violations and mass protests in Burma/Myanmar, pristine tourist beaches in Thailand, or tsunami waves swallowing those same beaches.

As with the other books in the Global Music Series, this book does not claim to be comprehensive of all the musical traditions of the region it covers. Rather, *Music in Mainland Southeast Asia* seeks to introduce some of the traditions from this area through an exploration of three themes that intersect with many of the musical communities of the peninsula. These themes—music and cultural diversity, music and political turmoil, and music and globalization—slice across the area, affording an opportunity to draw parallels and contrasts between different communities. The three musical issues that run through this text surely span the globe. Yet these issues provide us a way of approaching the complicated musical worlds of mainland Southeast Asia that embed musical practice in daily life.

Burma/Myanmar, Thailand, Laos, Cambodia, and Vietnam are extremely diverse in their ethnic, political, religious, and economic make-up. With over a hundred different languages and even more musical styles a survey of all the culture groups and music traditions across the mainland would fill many books. Each of the countries under discussion has suffered significant political turmoil over the past sixty years. The roots of this strife are numerous: the ethnic diversity of the area and the power sharing struggles between groups; the legacies of colonial interests that reorganized local economies; ideological struggles, clashing political ideologies, and a wide variety of government types—monarchy, communism, democracy.

Thailand has been open to researchers for many years and scholars have amassed a large body of literature. Laos, Cambodia, Vietnam, and Burma/Myanmar, in contrast, have been variously restricted to researchers over the past few decades. In the past ten years access has greatly improved and indigenous scholarship has also begun to circulate.

To engage the task of introducing you to this complex area I will deal primarily with four countries that stretch across the mainland: Burma/Myanmar, Thailand, Cambodia, and Vietnam. Laos will enter into the discussion in several situations, but my direct experience with that country has been limited. While any in-depth discussion of Malaysia and Singapore is beyond the scope of this project, their economic, religious, theatrical, and musical influence is significant. Malaysia's musical landscape constitutes a wide variety of traditions that find kinship with both Indonesian and Thai music particularly in the theatrical realm.

My primary fieldwork research has been in Burma/Myanmar, pursuing an interest very much driven by a combination of musical and political questions. During the mid-1990s when I first started researching Burmese music and culture there were fewer than ten commercial recordings available in the West and only a handful of articles written in English on the music. The music sounded unlike anything I had heard before (CD track 6 and track 9). Not like Chinese music and not like Indian music.

Why was so little known about this country? With so many recordings, books, articles, etc. available about its neighbors India, China, and Thailand, why had Burma/Myanmar fallen off the world map? And by what name was I to refer to it? A quick bit of research revealed not only music unlike any of those neighbors, but also a unique political situation. The dictatorship that had tried for years to keep the world out was now inviting much of the world in—at least in the form of business and tourism. I first arrived in the country in 1998, a few years after some significant policy and personnel changes in the government—changes that were to have a significant effect on certain musical traditions. Political questions continued to inform research for my graduate work in ethnomusicology. Why, I asked throughout my PhD dissertation, has Burma's bankrupt military dictatorship suddenly increased its funding and patronage of the traditional arts? More specifically, in what way does such patronage benefit the ruling junta and what are the consequences for artists? Some of those findings I will share with you in the following pages.

Over the years, with subsequent visits back to Southeast Asia, many of my questions have spilled into neighboring countries. Visiting Cambodia in 2003 I sought to compare and contrast with Burma/Myanmar some experiences of Khmer musicians dealing with histories of colonialism, war, corrupt governments, and the forces of globalization. What similarities can be found across these experiences and how are they substantively different? How, further, do they contrast with musical communities in Thailand who did not deal with overt colonial forces yet had no shortage of political turmoil? Vietnam, in many musical and cultural ways, stands distinct from the rest of mainland Southeast Asia, yet in regard to the themes set forth for this book, it offers some fascinating comparative case studies and reminds us of the fact that nation-state and historical boundaries are not as rigid as the maps on our walls would suggest.

Though contemporary nation-states exert an extremely strong influence on cultural behavior and provide an appropriate starting place for consideration of the area, we must remember that they are, all in all, a rather recent invention. Many linguistic groups, ethnic communities, and musical traditions predate the present national boundaries. National musics—musics that have come to be understood as representative of a country—may, therefore, not be reflective of the traditions and people inside the borders. Terms like Thai, Khmer, and Burmese reflect to some degree the nation-states of Thailand, Cambodia, and Myanmar but in many ways fall dreadfully short of accurately representing the people within the borders. Thus, a distinction must always be kept in mind between association with an ethnic group (Burmese music, Thai music, Khmer music) and the music in a particular country (music in Thailand, music in Vietnam, music of Myanmar).

ACTIVITY 1.2 *Locate a variety of political and geographical maps of Southeast Asia online or in the library.*

Download from the Internet a blank, unlabeled map of Southeast Asia.

Starting from the map in Figure 1.1 find and label on your map major cities: Mandalay, Yangon, Bangkok, Chiang Mai,

Vientiane, Siem Riep, Phnom Phen, Hanoi, Ho Chi Minh City. Note that their names may have a variety of different spellings.

From the additional maps you have found, find and label the countries that neighbor Southeast Asia: China, India, Bangladesh, Malaysia, The Philippines, Singapore, Indonesia.

Find and label the cites of the former empires: Hue, Angkor, Luang Prabang, Pagan, Sukothai, Ayutthaya.

Find and label the major rivers: Irrawaddy, Cao Phraya, Mekong, Salween, Red River.

CULTURAL INFLUENCES ON SOUTHEAST ASIA

This area of Asia has been subject to layer after layer of influence from both nearby and far away. Many of these histories are locally acknowledged and embraced while others may be contested, denied, or challenged by local or national interests. Despite the claims of many heritage organizations and government doctrines we cannot speak of cultural or ethnic purity in this region, as no country is homogenous in its ethnic makeup or its historical lineage.

The history of cultural influences includes not only the transplantation of material goods, behaviors, ideas, and styles but also the active reinterpretation and adaptation of influences into the local context. Vietnamese instruments, largely originating in China, are adjusted to bend and shape notes conforming to the Vietnamese aesthetic rather than the Chinese. Pianos, adopted in Burma during the British colonial period, were approached originally with a two-finger, 7-tone style (no black keys) drawn from performance practice on the indigenous *pat-tala* (xylophone). Performances of the Ramayana, the great Hindu epic from India, are found throughout the region, enacted in many local versions that are distinct from each other and from Indian versions. The Vietnamese language has incorporated many Chinese loan words; likewise Burmese, Lao, Khmer, and Thai languages are permeated with Sanskrit and Pali words from India.

The European term "Indochina" applied to this area reflects the prominence of Indian and Chinese influences upon this region that stretch back over two thousand years. Ancient Indian and Chinese influences such as Hindu, Buddhist, Confucian, and Taoist philosophies have been interpreted and adapted in such specific ways that Indian and Chinese visitors to the area today would likely feel out of place.

Contact between India and Southeast Asia began over 2000 years ago primarily for reasons of trade and religious expansion. Those people living in the margins—at higher elevations or deep in remote jungles—were usually the last to be affected by these economic and religious campaigns. Indian civilization had a significant impact not only in terms of religious and philosophical traditions but a wide variety of other practices including architecture, sculpture, language, literature, agricultural practices, dance, puppetry, and, of course, music.

While Indian influence is most prominent in Burma/Myanmar, Thailand, and Cambodia, the Chinese influence in Vietnam is most evident. Unlike the Indian relations with Southeast Asia, which were mostly peaceful, Chinese involvement with Vietnam (and to a lesser degree the other countries) was often adversarial and colonial. Despite the aggressively resisted colonial and military campaigns from the north, however, Vietnam did adopt many aspects of Chinese culture including writing and Mahayana Buddhism—a variety of Buddhism distinct from the Theravada sect found throughout most of the peninsula. I will return to these different Buddhisms shortly.

PRESENT DAY NATION-STATES

While foreign influence has impacted mainland Southeast Asia for thousands of years, recent nation-state formation, political struggle, ethnic identity assertion, and global media have also had a profound impact on the region. The pre-modern history of the region is deep and complex and informs much of the contemporary political and cultural organization (see Figure 1.5). Brief accounts of the countries in the area will set the stage for contemporary comparison.

Burma/Myanmar (Union of Myanmar).

Population: 48 Million

Capital: Nay Pyi Taw (administrative capital, 2006)

Major Cities: Yangon (Rangoon), Mandalay, Mawlamyine, Taunggyi

Government: Military Dictatorship

Major ethnic groups: Burman 68%, Shan 9%, Karen 7%, Rakhine 4%, Chinese 3% Indian 2%, Mon 2%, Chin, Kachin, and others (135 official ethnicities)

Name	Century	Area
Champa	2–15th	central Vietnam
Dvaravati/Mon	6–11th	Thailand
Pyu	6–11th	Burma/Myanmar
Srivijawa	6–13th	Indonesia
Sailendras	8–9th	Indonesia, Malaysia, S. Thailand
Pegu/Mon	9–11th	Burma/Myanmar
Pagan	11–13th	Burma/Myanmar
Sukhothai	13–14th	Thailand
Lan Na	13–16th	north Thailand
Ayutthaya	14–18th	Thailand

FIGURE 1.5 *Empires and Kingdoms in Southeast Asia.*

Burma/Myanmar is the western most country in mainland Southeast Asia. Bordered by India and Bangladesh to the west, China to the north, and Thailand and Laos to the east, it stretches 1200 miles from the snowy Himalayan range to the tropical waters of the Andaman Sea. Early empires could be found on the territory with the Pyu in the 1st century BCE, the Mon in the 9th century and the 11th century, and the first Burmese empire founded under King Anawrahta in the 11th century. The nation-state of Burma took its present borders under British colonialism. Through three wars (1823–26, 1852, 1867) the British eventually took administrative control over Burma/Myanmar. After 1868, Burma was annexed to India, the neighboring British colony, and in 1937 it became a separately administrated colonial territory. Burma was a major theater in WWII between the Allied (British and American) forces and the Japanese. A growing independence movement throughout the 1930s and 40s convinced many Burmese to side with whichever force (British or Japanese) would grant them independence. Independence hero General Aung San fought first with the Japanese and later with the British. He laid the groundwork for independence by enlisting the trust of many of the disparate ethnic minorities—unifying the diverse country to push out the British. Aung San, however, was assassinated by a political rival in 1947, just months before the scheduled independence day of January 4th 1948.

The newly independent Burma struggled with post WWII recon-struction, shaky leadership, and civil wars with ethnic insurgents, which eventually led to a take-over by the military (under General Ne Win) in 1962. Rather than working to integrate the new nation into the post-WWII world, the Ne Win regime chose isolation, leading to a sharp decrease in trade, tourism, and political dialogue (as well as musical exchange) with Burma's neighbors and the rest of the world. By 1988, with the economy in shambles, a student-led revolution (known as the 8-8-88 revolution for the auspicious date that it commenced) took to the streets, demanding political and economic reform.

Aung San Suu Kyi, daughter of independence hero Aung San, had returned to Burma from her home in England to care for her aged mother. Aung San Suu Kyi soon became involved in the country's dia-logue for change and ran for office (as the head of the National League for Democracy party) in the 1990 elections promised by the governing generals. The military was threatened by the public support for Suu Kyi, however, and placed her under house arrest several months prior to the election. Although the election results overwhelmingly supported the NLD, the results were not honored. Aung San Suu Kyi has spent most of the years since 1990 under house arrest and has been recognized inter-nationally numerous times for her peaceful will for change, not the least of which was the Nobel Prize for peace in 1991.

The public demonstration of Buddhist monks against the regime in September of 2007 (see Chapters 4 and 5) received worldwide attention yet did not lead to substantive political change. In 2009, the military regime (the SPDC-State Peace and Development Council) retains power, and Aung San Suu Kyi is still under house arrest. "Myanmar" is the official name of the country, although many prodemocracy groups (and Aung San Suu Kyi herself) claim that the 1989 name-change was ille-gal and have resisted its adoption. This controversial name change was recognized by the United Nations and by countries such as France and Japan, but not by the United States or the United Kingdom. The name of the country remains contentious, thus, I refer to the nation as Burma/Myanmar.

Thailand (Kingdom of Thailand).

Population: 65 Million

Capital: Bangkok

Major Cities: Bangkok, Nonthaburi, Pak Kret, Hat Yai, Chiang Mai

Government: Constitutional Monarchy

Major Ethnic Groups: Thai 75%, Chinese 14%, Malay, Mon, Khmer, and others

To the east of Burma/Myanmar, the southwest of Laos and west of Cambodia we find Thailand. Unlike the other countries in the mainland of Southeast Asia, Thailand was never a colony of a European power. It has had long histories of exchange (musical, cultural, military, etc.) with both the Burmese and the Khmer empires, and more recently with European and Asian powers. Formerly known as Siam, the first state is generally considered to have been the kingdom of Sukhothai. This Buddhist kingdom was founded in 1238 coinciding with the decline and fall of the Khmer Kingdom (13th–15th centuries) of present day Cambodia (see below). By the mid 14th century Khmer power diminished as the Thai kingdom of Ayutthaya flourished—until Ayutthaya was sacked by the Burmese in 1767. Shortly after, the capital was moved to Bangkok and today's Chakri dynasty began under King Rama I (1782–1809). During the colonial era Siam remained a neutral buffer state between the British colony of Burma and the French Indochinese colonies of Laos, Cambodia, and Vietnam (see Figure 1.1). It was during this period, with Thailand pressured from British interests to the West and French ones to the East that King Chulalongkorn (1868–1910), discussed in detail below, instituted a multitude of reforms that would facilitate Thailand's engagement with the Western world and with various globalizing forces. Some of the most significant reforms included the abolition of slavery, retooling of the national educational system to embrace Western science and, ultimately democratic ideals. In 1932 a revolution removed the absolute power of the kingship as the country developed a constitutional monarchy.

Throughout much of World War II Thailand was occupied by the armed forces of the Empire of Japan. During this occupation the "Death Railway" was constructed, linking Bangkok to Rangoon (now Yangon) and including the famous Bridge on the River Kwai. The railway was built using the labor of Allied Prisoners of War and slaves from the Thai citizenry.

In the post-WWII era, Thailand has struggled with multiple coups d'état with one military regime replacing another. Despite its continued openness to foreign tourism and business the instability of the government continues with the most recent coup occuring in 2006 and civil uprisings against the current government in the news as this book goes to press. The current monarch, His Majesty Bhumibol Adulyadej (Rama IX) ascended the throne in 1946 and is the world's longest reigning monarch.

Cambodia (Kingdom of Cambodia).

Population: 14 Million

Capital: Phnom Penh

Major Cites: Phnom Penh, Battambang, Siem Reap, and Tbeng Mean Chey

Government: Multiparty democracy under a constitutional monarchy

Major Ethnic Groups: Khmer 90%, Vietnamese 5%, Chinese 1%, Cham < 1%

East of Thailand and west of Vietnam lies Cambodia. To trace the history of Cambodia, one needs to hark back to the Khmer empire. The Khmer people absorbed many aspects of the previous Indic cultures (Founan and Champa) that controlled the areas including Hinduism and the concept of the *deva raja*: "god king." Hinduism was one of the first Khmer empire's official religions as developed by King Jayavarman II (802–830). Angkor Wat was the center of Hindu, Mahayana Buddhist, and Theravada Buddhist practice throughout the Angkor period. During the 11th century, the Khmer Empire, under Suryavarman I (1002–1050) expanded into parts of what is now Thailand and Laos and the northern half of the Malay Peninsula. During this period the Khmer Empire became powerful and much energy was devoted to temple construction. The great temple complex of Angkor Wat and the myriad temples and shrines in the area date from this period, and much of it still stands today. The design of Angkor Wat (and many related shrines) is modeled on Mt. Meru, the mythical mountain at the center of the universe around which the continents and oceans are ordered. Detailed bas-reliefs on the temple walls show many aspects of Khmer culture from this period, including depictions of dance, musical performance, and instruments (see Figures 1.6 and 1.7).

The rise of the *Tai* kingdoms of Sukhothai (1238) and Ayutthaya (1350) led to numerous wars with the Khmer kingdom, culminating in the destruction of much of Angkor in 1431. "*Tai*" here refers to the ethnolinguistic group in contrast to the "Thai" nation (largely made up of *Tai* people). The *Tai* returned to Ayutthaya with ninety thousand prisoners, many of whom were dancers and musicians, and would bring Khmer music sensibilities to the growing Thai court. Angkor, abandoned to the jungle, was left in decline with the capital moving to Phnom Penh in 1434. Siamese and Vietnamese aggression over the

FIGURE 1.6   *An apsara (celestial) dancer carved into the walls of Angkor Wat.*

following centuries led Cambodia to appeal to France for protection in 1863. Thus, it became a French protectorate in 1864. For the next century France dominated Cambodia commercially as part of the Indochinese Union (with Vietnam and Laos) until independence in 1949. The majority ethnic group living in Cambodia today is the Khmer. In the Khmer language the country was traditionally called Kampuchea. From 1975 to 1979 the country was ruled by the Khmer Rouge and named Democratic Kampuchea. Because of the Khmer Rouge's horrific "reign of terror", the term Kampuchea is now generally avoided when referring to the country in English. The Khmer people are closely related to the Mon who,

FIGURE 1.7   *Angkor Wat, Cambodia.*

after migrating south from China, settled further to the west in present day Burma two millennia ago.

The Cold War, the Vietnam War, and numerous internal political struggles combined to create a chaotic life for many Khmer during the second half of the 20th century. Led by Pol Pot (Saloth Sar), the Khmer Rouge set the 1975 calendar to year zero and forcibly returned the country to an agrarian economy. Estimates claim that 1–3 million people (or 1/4 to 1/3 of the country's population) died during Pol Pot's rule. 90% of Cambodia's musicians and artists were killed or starved to death.

After the brutality of the 1970s and 1980s and the near total destruction of Cambodia's cultural, economic, and political life, reconstruction is underway and political stability has largely returned. The present Cambodian King and head of state is Norodom Sihamoni was trained in Cambodian classical dance and taught dance in Paris. Prior to ascending to the throne he choreographed and directed his own dance company.

Vietnam (Socialist Republic of Vietnam).

Population: 85 Million

Capital: Hanoi

Major Cites: Hanoi, Hué, Ho Chi Minh City, Danang, Nha Trang, Dalat

Government: Communist State

Major Ethnic Groups: Kinh (Việt) 86%, Tay 2%, Thai 2%, Muong 1.5%, Khome 1.4%, Hoa 1.1%, Nun 1.1%, Hmong 1%

The Socialist Republic of Vietnam stretches along the East Coast of mainland Southeast Asia from China and the Gulf of Tonkin in the north to Cambodia and the Gulf of Thailand in the south with a western border shared with Laos (Figure 1.1). While these borders were established in the 1600s after a long process of southern expansion and migration, the narrow, elongated shape of the country (over 3000 km long and as narrow as 50 km in spots) has contributed to great diversity and regionalism. Vietnam has 59 provinces, which can be grouped into three cultural regions: the north, center, and south, each with a distinct language or dialect, music and culture.

The population of Vietnam is currently 85 million and is characterized by a high degree of cultural diversity (officially 54 ethnic groups). The largest of the ethnic groups (the Việt or Kinh) lives in the lowland areas along the Pacific coast and in the deltas of the Mekong and Red Rivers. Other ethnic groups live primarily in the highlands that border China, Laos, and Cambodia. Unlike in Burma/Myanmar, Thailand, and Cambodia it is impossible to define a distinctly Vietnamese national music. Even the music of the majority group shows strong regional differences.

The French began to colonize parts of southern Vietnam in the 1860s. The Vietnamese monarchy lost most of its power to the French in 1884, but a long resistance movement characterized the relationship between the French and the Vietnamese. In 1930 a nationalist movement staged an uprising against the French, and Hồ Chí Minh organized the Indochinese Communist party. Under Hồ Chí Minh's leadership the newly declared Democratic Republic of Vietnam fought against Japanese occupation during WWII and led the communists in a guerilla war against the French, culminating in the defeat of the French in 1954. Vietnam was then divided at the 17th parallel into two separate north/south countries with the communists controlling the north. Northern communists continued to pursue the eradication of French and foreign influences in their cities.

In 1964 the United States intervened, aiming to preserve a non-communist south, while the communist north supported by Russia and China continued its aggression south. During the conflict, approximately 3 to 4 million Vietnamese on both sides were killed, in addition to another 1.5 to 2 million Lao and Cambodians who were drawn into the war. Strong division in America about involvement in Vietnam led to the gradual withdrawal of troops beginning in 1969. South Vietnam and Saigon fell to the communists in 1975. Over one million people fled Vietnam, leading to the development of diasporic Vietnamese communities throughout the world.

ORGANIZING MAINLAND SOUTHEAST ASIA

Organizing the discussion of mainland Southeast Asia is a challenge. Perhaps the most obvious way is nation-state by nation-state, as I have presented in the previous section. One of the primary directives of the government of any nation-state is national unity. Through common laws, educational systems, trade infrastructure, print and televised media, and other methods, governments simultaneously cultivate an impression of shared values among those living within its borders and project to outsiders and other governments an image of a coherent whole. The construction of national identities has been one of the more forceful agents of cultural change in Southeast Asia over the past century. National identities provide one set of categories for organizing the socio-cultural worlds of the region. But they are not the only ways to think about and categorize life in the area.

Other ways that we might consider life in the region are through the categories of highland/lowland, rural/urban, and ethnicity. Many of the major historical empires in the area were situated in lowland valleys where large-scale rice cultivation could support large cities and attract large numbers of people. These great civilizations in Southeast Asia were located along rivers, deltas and coastal areas. Such cities were much more homogeneous linguistically but were highly stratified socially and could support not only armies and kings but also artists, craftsmen, dancers, and musicians, who would support the elite sectors of the society. In contrast, the rugged mountains of northern Burma/Myanmar that stretch into the Himalayas, the jungled highlands of Laos, and the dense hills of Thailand, Cambodia, and Vietnam are home to many peoples whose way of life, even today, is radically different from those in the lowland. The upland communities generally had much more diversity in language—a result of smaller communities living in areas where travel and trade was difficult. Also these areas are characterized by greater political fragmentation and diverse and agricultural practices.

> **ACTIVITY 1.3** *Find a topographical map of Southeast Asia. Note the elevation changes and where the urban centers and historical cities are located in this regard. Revisit your maps from activity 1.2. Go back and label mountainous areas, jungle areas, and deltas.*

While many countries throughout Asia today have extremely dense populations, Southeast Asia has historically had much lower population densities, especially compared to China, India, or Japan. Rapid development over the past century and the industrialization of many economies has encouraged migration to urban centers. Major cities like Bangkok (9 million), Ho Chi Minh City (7 million), Yangon/Rangoon (6 million), and Hanoi (3 million) have grown at a rapid pace over the past several decades. Bangkok, for example, barely had 1 million residents at the end of WWII. The pace of such urban growth (averaging 3–3.5% a year in most large cities) strongly influences cultural forms, as different cultures (ethnicities, languages, religions) come into greater contact with each other and relations with the global economy are fostered and developed through urban business. National and international immigrant communities move to the large cities, often for work opportunities, while large populations still live in the rural areas—often supported by family members making money in the city.

Religion in Mainland Southeast Asia. Another perspective we might take on the region is by religion. I have emphasized in this chapter the multiple diverse cultural influences both historically and in contemporary times from neighboring countries and from abroad. I have also pointed out the wide varieties of ethnic and religious communities; for example, in vignette 2 I introduced the coexistence of multiple belief systems. Indeed, the religious traditions found in Southeast Asia are many and varied with representation of all the world's major religions found throughout the area. As elsewhere in the world, these religious traditions provide a lens for examining local musics, and the musics can help us learn about these local beliefs systems.

The sounds of religious behavior in many areas of Southeast Asia are the sounds of the community, not marginalized to simply religious space. In Burma/Myanmar one can stand on the steps of a famous Buddhist shrine—the Sule Pagoda in downtown Yangon—and hear prayer bells chime and monks chanting *sutras* (see below) into microphones amplified on overdriven loudspeakers. If you sit long enough you'll hear across the street to the east the bells of Immanuel Baptist Church ringing to invite the Christian community to worship. Or, if you listen to the west, the Muslim call to prayer can be heard from loudspeakers at the Cholia Jama Mosque. A short walk from the Sule Pagoda can also take you to several Hindu temples, a Catholic church or a Sikh temple. Religious diversity is part of the urban environment and religious sound is part of the urban soundscape in many of Southeast Asia's major cities. Even in Vietnam where numerous individuals self-identify as non-religious, many visit temples for yearly festivals and to mark special occasions. Vietnamese traditions of ancestor worship, along with high reverence for national heroes, mix with Buddhist, Confucian, and Daoist beliefs.

In modern Thailand and Burma, both in the cities and in rural areas, many homes will have erected a spirit house in the corner of the garden. Animism or spirit worship is often accompanied by ritual chants and dances, special folk drama, or masques such as the shadow play. Underlying Buddhism throughout much of Burma/Myanmar and northern Thailand is animism—a belief that many things in the natural environment, such as trees, stones and rivers, have living souls. Spirit houses outside many buildings are made attractive to any possibly harmful spirit so that it will not haunt the humans living nearby. Buddhism has managed to mold itself onto animism throughout much of the region, producing an unusual blend of philosophies into a singular worldview. While scholars have debated the relationship between animistic traditions (supernatural beings like the *nat* in Burma or *phi* in Thailand) as two distinct religions, emphasis on the total worldview of practitioners (who actively engage with both of these seemingly disparate traditions) dissolves the contradiction (See Tambiah 1970, Keyes 1995).

As will be discussed in later chapters the influence of other global traditions has also had an impact on the religious and musical life of

Southeast Asian peoples. Large communities of Christian, Muslim, Hindu, Jewish, Baha'i, and others are found throughout the region and, while in the minority in each country, often play a significant role in local politics and in musical change.

Despite the rich diversity in religious traditions I would like here to shift to a commonality found throughout much of the Southeast Asian mainland region—the overwhelming presence of Buddhism in general (with specific attention paid to the Theravada sect of Buddhism)—and various monastic approaches to music. The Theravada tradition is practiced throughout Burma/Myanmar, Thailand, Laos and Cambodia. The dominance of the Mahayana tradition that is found throughout Vietnam speaks to the north south relations between Vietnam and China. I will address this further below.

Theravada Buddhism. Throughout Southeast Asia Buddhism, like Islam and Christianity, is mixed with indigenous rites and beliefs, and is found in a multitude of variations. Buddhism encompasses a rich array of traditions that have developed across Asia over the past 2500 years. Buddhism originated with the teachings and life lessons of Siddhartha Gautama (ca. 563 to 483 BCE) who is revered as the Buddha or the Enlightened One. As with other near-global traditions, Buddhism has been adapted and changed to accommodate local customs and it is found in many different forms and variations (see Fig 1.8). It is, thus, often difficult to recognize similarities across traditions as they are practiced. Some basic features shared by all varieties of Buddhism include the recognition of Siddhartha Gautama's great renunciation and his subsequent quest for and attainment of enlightenment, discussed further below.

Siddhartha Gautama was born in the 6th century BCE in ancient India inside the borders of present day Nepal. He was a prince who wanted for nothing and was destined to inherit his father's kingdom. At the age of twenty-nine Siddhartha ventured outside of the protective palace to witness the world first hand. His encounters with an elderly man, a diseased man, a decaying corpse and, finally, a monk or ascetic, led him to contemplate the nature of existence. Reflection on old age, disease, and unavoidable death led him to conclude that all life is suffering. Horrified by these revelations, Siddhartha left his palace late at night, abandoned his kingdom, his riches, his wife and child, and his line to the throne in search of a path to free all living creatures from this endless suffering.

For a time, Siddhartha chose the life of a wandering ascetic collecting alms for his food and eventually pursuing a regime of extreme abstinence from worldly things. Known as "the great struggle," this extreme practice reduced his body to skin and bones. The Buddha-to-be ultimately recognized this to be an ineffective way to escape suffering, and ultimately found the Middle Path. This middle path towards

(a)

FIGURE 1.8a and b *a) The Shwedagon Pagoda, Burma/Myanmar; b) Buddhas in Ayutthaya, Thailand.*

Reverence for the Buddha is reflected throughout Southeast Asia through the construction of stupas and Buddha images. Stupas, or pagodas, are shrines in the shape of the mythical center of the universe Mount Mehru, in which are contained various bodily relics of the Buddha (a tooth fragment or a hair, for example). These sites, and the numerous Buddha images that are usually found at them, are reminders of the Buddha's humanity and serve as primary spaces for rituals and meditation.

(b)

FIGURE 1.8 *continued*

realizing the true nature of reality travels between the extremes of self-indulgence and self-mortification.

Siddhartha concluded that the root of our suffering is to be found in our attachment to the world—to our communities, to material wealth, to our families, to our bodies, and selves. He journeyed to Bodha Gaya in northeast India, sat cross-legged under a bodhi tree and meditated. Despite many temptations by worldly desires, through meditation he became aware of the *Dharma*—the truth or law of human existence. This was the beginning of his enlightenment—the wisdom of emptiness. At this point he became the Buddha—the Enlightened One.

Common to all Buddhist traditions are the Four Noble Truths taught by the Buddha. The "Four Noble Truths" was the first sermon given by Gautama Buddha after his enlightenment.

1. Life is suffering.
2. The origin of suffering is attachment.
3. The cessation of suffering is attainable.
4. The path to the cessation of suffering is the noble eightfold path which consists of right view, right intention, right speech, right

action, right livelihood, right effort, right mindfulness, right concentration.

In Asia today there are several traditions of Buddhism. The most prominent division is between the Mahayana tradition found in northern areas (China, Japan, Korea and Vietnam) and the Theravada tradition found in southern countries (Sri Lanka, Burma/Myanmar, Thailand, Cambodia and Laos). As you can see, the Theravada tradition is dominant in mainland Southeast Asia, with Vietnam and many of the immigrant Chinese communities (especially in Singapore) practicing Mahayana Buddhism.

The Mahayana tradition, referred to by many as the Great Vehicle, is generally regarded as the more ritualistic and cosmological. The great 9th century monument of Borobudur in Java (Sailendra dynasty) is evidence of the deep historical roots of Mahayana Buddhism in Southeast Asia. Mahayana rituals have adopted many local practices over the centuries in contrast to the comparatively more uniform Theravada rituals. The role of music in many Mahayana traditions is significant as music can be used as an offering, as an aid for meditation and as a pedagogical tool. In Theravada traditions music as a direct offering is somewhat less frequent, though, as noted above at the Erawan Shrine (vignette 1), it does occur.

In mainland Southeast Asia the dominant Theravada tradition has had enormous influence on cultural behavior of all forms. In addition to recognizing the Buddha and his teachings (the Dharma/Dhamma) the Theravada tradition emphasizes the preservation of the past in the actual practices and the actual words of the Buddha. Theravada Buddhism is often referred to as "The Way of the Elders" a title that reflects the reverence for tradition and particular practices. Respect for elders has significant impact in all aspects of Theravada-informed culture, as we shall see in the traditional music (see Wong 2001).

Theravada practice strongly emphasizes the texts associated with the Buddha recorded in the Pali language. Pali is the Indian language of the earliest extant Buddhist texts and is the language in which all Theravada liturgy is practiced—whether in Burma/Myanmar, Thailand, or Cambodia. Monks across these countries share the same liturgy and study and practice across borders. Due to this emphasis on text (the actual words of the Buddha, as remembered and recorded by his disciples after his death) and on specific practices, Theravada is regarded as the more conservative tradition but also the one with perceived direct links to the actual Buddha. The shared philosophies, cosmologies, views on enlightenment, texts, and histories provide a common set of principles for Theravada Buddhists throughout Southeast Asia and in immigrant communities around the world.

ACTIVITY 1.4   *Find the nearest Buddhist center or monastery in your community. Can you visit them? Phone or email them. Many will have websites and email addresses and my experiences suggest that most will be very welcoming of visitors.*

If you visit explore these questions:
What type of Buddhism is practiced?
How did the monks come to be there?
What community does it serve (i.e., a particular nationality or ethnicity, immigrants, etc.)?
What sort of relationship could you assess between the community and the monks?
Are there any festivals that are celebrated at this facility?
What role does music play in rituals or in social events?
Describe the physical space.

Write a paper or prepare a short report to your class.

In Burma/Myanmar, Thailand, and Cambodia, where upwards of 90% of the population is actively engaged in Theravada Buddhism, an intimate relationship exists between the laity (the supporting community) and the order of Buddhist monks known as the *sangha*. Most men in the Theravada tradition will, at one or more points in their life, be initiated into the monkhood (Figure 1.9). Monk initiation involves a complex set of rituals that re-enact Siddhartha's renunciation of the world. Tenure in the Theravada monastery may last for a short period or much longer: three weeks, three months, or in fewer cases, a lifetime. Once initiated, a man who practices the rites for three weeks is no less a monk than one who has practiced for three years. Short stays in the monastery contrasts significantly with vows in many Christian monastic traditions that for most are taken for life. This constant exchange between monastic and lay personnel forges a unique relationship between the community and the local monastery. Each is supported by the other in an economically, politically, and spiritually symbiotic relationship. The laity depends upon monks for spiritual guidance and officiance over various rituals; the *sangha* depends upon the laity for donations of food, robes, and maintenance of the monastery.

Theravada Buddhist Chant.   In most Theravada monasteries, ritual time and daily lifeways are in great measure signaled and structured through sonic practices such as the patterned sounding of log drums,

(a)

FIGURE 1.9a and b   *Monk Initiation in Myanmar (before and after). The five males in the photo above are joining the monastery (called a shin byu in Burma/ Myanmar). Note the two young males, first time initiates, dressed in royal clothing enacting the royal station of Siddhartha dressed in royal clothes (see Hla Pe 1985). Later that day, as seen in the photo to the right, they have shed their civilian and royal clothes, shaved their heads and are taking vows.*

(b)

FIGURE 1.9   *continued*

bells or gongs, and chant. However, as in some other religious traditions throughout the world (see Marcus 2007 in this series) one finds in
Theravada Buddhism precepts that forbid engagement with music, on
the grounds that it is inappropriate to the habits of someone pursuing
a religious life. The Seventh of the Ten Buddhist precepts, adopted by
all in the *sangha*, asserts that one should refrain from dancing, singing,
music, and theater. This requirement is generally said to apply only to
the monks and to devout lay people.

  In practice, the principle has many interpretations. The general
consensus turns on the degree of distraction that such activity creates from the religious pathway. Further understandings of the sonic

practice of monastic chant points to a different way of conceptualizing the sounds, thereby creating a distinction between chant and music. While Buddhist chant may sound like "music" it is often not referred to as such in the monasteries (CD track 4). One can readily find monks in the Theravada world who refute the assertion that their chanting is "music" or "singing." In contrast, during my own fieldwork in Burma/ Myanmar, Thailand, and Cambodia I frequently met monks (senior monks at that) who wanted to discuss music with me and even invited me into their monasteries to make recordings with local musicians. I frequently accepted this invitation, as monasteries were often much quieter locations than the tightly packed homes adjacent to bustling street noise at which many musicians and teachers lived. One can surely find monasteries where the approaches to music are both more liberal and more orthodox.

As the Theravada tradition places a strong emphasis on the original Pali text, the resultant sound of Theravada chant—in comparison to many Chinese, Japanese, or Tibetan Buddhist chants—is quite conservative in its expression. Rhythm is steady and often phrased around the line of text, pitch variety is usually quite limited, ornamentation is restricted, and the presentation of the text is very syllabic (i.e., one note per syllable). Text is paramount and should always be accessible to the listener.

ACTIVITY 1.5   *Listen several times to the example of Buddhist chant on CD track 4. Listen again, to discern how many notes there are for each syllable of text. Though I do not expect you to understand Pali, the clear enunciation of the text should be apparent. This is a "syllabic" style of text setting. Notice also the phrasing of each line of text with its "sung" ending. Try and pick out the pitches and sing along using any syllables you wish or even humming.*

Chant in the Theravada monastic context serves multiple purposes for both the *sangha* (the order of monks) and the laity. It serves as prayer, as meditation and as a form of protection. Chanting may be done solo but is usually conducted in a group setting as heard on CD track 4, where large portions of the Pali text are collectively rehearsed and memorized. The memorization of texts consumes a large portion of any monk's time, and is a mark of education and authority among senior monks.

As I will show in Chapter 2, this chant style contrasts with many of the "classical" and "courtly" music traditions of mainland Southeast Asia. As you have heard, when Theravada chant is done in large groups all participants follow the identical text, melody, and rhythm with no individual or distinct music parts. As with the Buddhist philosophy behind the chant, the self (in this case the individual voice) is regarded not as an individual but simply as part of the whole, a part of something greater. This contrasts with many classical musics from the region that have either a soloistic style or a small ensemble music quality with little in the way of doubling of instruments and little unison synchronicity of parts.

The Three Gems. Chanting serves as prayer, as mediation, and as a form of spiritual and physical protection. While there is some degree of variation and emphasis in different texts throughout the region, there are some text that are found throughout the Theravada world. One of these is "The Three Refuges" also known as the "Three Jewels" or "The Three Gems." The three gems are the three things that all Buddhists surrender themselves to and in return look to for guidance. This is known as taking refuge. A practicing Buddhist seeks refuge in the Buddha (the historical figure and model), the *dhamma* (the teachings and lessons of the Buddha), and the *sangha* (the monks that maintain and preserve the tradition).

Recitation of the three gems, an activity that begins many meetings between lay people and monks, is sung in Pali and consists of a thrice-repeated iteration of the refuge. You should be able to follow the text of CD track 5 easily.

The Three Gems

Buddham saranam gacchāmi	I go for refuge in the Buddha
Dhammam saranam gacchāmi	I go for refuge in the Dhamma
Sangham saranam gacchāmi	I go for refuge in the Sangha
Dutiyampi buddham saranam gacchāmi	For the second time, I go for refuge in the Buddha
Dutiyampi dhammam saranam gacchāmi	For the second time, I go for refuge in the Dhamma

Dutiyampi sangham saranam gacchāmi	For the second time, I go for refuge in the Sangha
Tatiyampi buddham saranam gacchāmi	For the third time, I go for refuge in the Buddha
Tatiyampi dhammam saranam gacchāmi	For the third time, I go for refuge in the Dhamma
Tatiyampi sangham saranam gacchāmi	For the third time, I go for refuge in the Sangha

The practice of chanting permeates many areas of Buddhist behavior and Buddhist ritual. Beyond taking refuge in the three gems, Buddhists often recite some of the words or *suttas/sutras* (Pali/Sanskrit) credited to the Buddha, for blessing and protection. These chants, always in Pali, are memorized and recited for numerous types of occasions where a ritual or social event requires a blessing or some form of shielding/ defense from misfortune, sickness, or evil spirits. For example, several weddings that I attended in Burma during my research each had moments where monks would recite *parritas* to bless and protect the young couple. While this might on the surface appear similar to the role of a priest/minister in a Christian wedding context, it is really quite different. Marriage is not a religious act in Buddhism (as it often is in Christianity); in fact it is quite the opposite, as it is very clearly a reflection of the worldly attachments that we have. A monk would not have a legal (worldly) role in legitimizing the union, as a priest would have in the West, but rather would bring protection and blessing to the union and would also reinforce the relationship between the laity and the *sangha*.

Paritta chants are also used for education. Monks sit with lay people and recite them in a responsorial manner with devotees repeating each line after the monks (similar to the responsorial recitation of the three gems on CD example 5). It is also common for monks to translate a *paritta* from the Pali into the local Burmese, Thai, or Khmer language for the people. *Paritta* chant, therefore, becomes a tool for educating lay-people about the *dhamma* (the teachings of the Buddha). In addition a few devout laypeople have studied and memorized *parittas* themselves. Rituals involving *paritta* chant interlock the religious needs of the lay people who seek blessings and protection from evil forces with the educational intents of the monks who seek to inspire mindfulness and to educate laypeople about the *dhamma* and to encourage the laity to memorize the Pali scriptures (Greene 2004, 71).

Throughout Theravada Buddhist Southeast Asia the relationship between the *sangha* and the laity, then, is quite intertwined. Most Buddhist males (and to some degree females) spend some time in the monasteries (and nunneries) and, in so doing, learn many chants and many of the *dhamma* lessons of the Buddha. Buddhist chant, while arguably not music to be enjoyed recreationally, is a primary conduit for the transmission of Buddhist teaching and for the education of the public at large. The *sangha*, chanting and memorizing as a group, are the guardians of the *dhamma*. Melodic recitation of the words of the Buddha aids in memorizing the text, emphasizes the actual words recited aloud, and has acted over the past centuries as a valuable system for the storage and retrieval of sacred texts. At the same time, through the coordinated efforts of the monks, unique individuality is lost as all pursue the ultimate goals of being born into a better life after rebirth.

Vietnamese Buddhism. In contrast to the Theravada traditions of Cambodia, Laos, Thailand, and Burma/Myanmar, the religious traditions of Vietnam are comparatively diverse. Mahayana Buddhism, Confucianism, and Taoism have long influenced the worldview of the Vietnamese. These religious and philosophical perspectives were fostered and developed through millennia of cultural exchange with China. This contrasts with the strong influence of Indian civilization over other parts of Southeast Asia.

As in mainland countries to the west, many local practices in Vietnam have been strongly influenced by a system of animistic beliefs that became integrated into the more formal religious institutions based in Buddhist temples. In stark contrast to other countries in the area, most Vietnamese do not self-identify with a particular religious tradition. Of the remainder there are numerous practitioners of Mahayana Buddhism with over one thousand temples nationwide and a former status as the national religion.

The Mahayana tradition reached Vietnam by the 3rd century AD and from the 10th century on flourished throughout Vietnam among all classes of people (Nguyen 2002). Vietnam's Buddhist ceremonies, texts and training share much with practices in China, Korea and Japan, yet due to different languages and musics, a visiting monk from one of these countries could only participate minimally. This also contrasts with Theravada traditions where the ritual language and chanting is quite similar across Sri Lanka, Burma/Myanmar, Thailand and

Cambodia. In Vietnam, Buddhist chanting varies regionally as well; no orthodox manner of chanting and singing is consistent throughout the country. While most of the Buddhist music in Vietnam is vocal, it can also be realized with musical instruments and can also include dance (Nguyen 2002). Compare that with the Theravada tradition, which is entirely vocal and does not include dance.

The doctrinal differences between the two Buddhist traditions consist of their differing views of Gautama Buddha. In the Mahayana school, Gautama is regarded as one of many "enlightened ones," manifesting the fundamental divine power of the universe. In the Theravada school Gautama is the one-and-only enlightened one and the great teacher, human and not divine.

ACTIVITY 1.6   *Explore the following website for examples of Buddhist chant.*

http://www.buddhanet.net/audio.htm

Compare and contrast examples from Mahayana and Theravada traditions. How many pitches can you hear in each chant style? Can you determine which style is syllabic and which includes more melismatic singing?

Compare and contrast examples from Thailand and Burma/ Myanmar.

How would you describe the use of melody, pitch, rhythm, and instrumentation in general?

Compare and contrast several recordings of the Three Gems.

CONCLUSION

The diversity of ethnicities and traditions across mainland Southeast Asia cannot be overstated. Such diversity often contradicts the borders imposed by empires, colonies, and nation-states. Common experiences across much of the peninsula can be found through the historical presence of Hinduism and Buddhism, most specifically of the Theravada variety. The common practices of Theravada Buddhist monk—chant, initiation, relation with laity—form one unifying behavioral feature of the area that underpins much of the secular musical practices. Buddhism has also played a significant role in the foundation of empires and kingship where much of the "classical" and "court" musics of the region were forged. It is to these traditions that I shall turn in Chapter 2.

Classical Traditions, Court Traditions, National Traditions

Chapters 2 and 3 will explore some types of musical diversity across mainland Southeast Asia. The breadth of diversity cannot be overstated; one could travel through the region for a lifetime and still fall short of exploring all of the traditions that exist in the area. I will begin by exploring several categories into which music might be organized. The themes of globalization and political turmoil will also make brief appearances as we discuss this diversity.

ACTIVITY 2.1   *Write down on three separate pieces of paper all of the musical characteristics and connotations that come to mind from the words "classical," "folk," and "popular." Don't stop until you have at least ten words on each list. Then do a mini-survey with two or three friends, asking them to do the same thing. Your next task is to analyze what you have collected, with the following questions:*

In what ways do these rubrics overlap? What characteristic sounds would you associate with each? What non-sonic associations or connotations are found with each? Can you think of a musical tradition that belongs in more than one (or all three) of the categories? Are there any musical traditions that don't fit in any of them? Why? Why Not? Can you think of a music tradition that has moved over time from one category to another?

Organize your materials into sonic (musical) characteristics and social or contextual characteristics.

> *Is there any consensus among you and your classmates as to what defines each type?*

WHAT IS "CLASSICAL" MUSIC IN SOUTHEAST ASIA?

The terms "classical music," "art music," and "court music" are all highly problematic in the context of Southeast Asian music. What makes certain traditions classical and others not is often unclear and might be different from one area to another. Furthermore, terms like "folk" and "popular," used to describe other musical traditions outside of the elite sphere, are equally problematic.

Musics called "classical" in the West are often associated with a social or economic elite. These musics are often symbolically associated by the elite with the nation (officially or not) and often regarded as a pinnacle (at least within the region) of aesthetic achievement. As you (hopefully) explored in Activity 2.1, these categories are not rigid and are often contingent more upon who is doing the labeling than upon any sonic characteristics. In this chapter I will present several traditions drawn from the royal courts, yet I must caution the reader from assuming that these musics represent all of the people in a particular country. The dilemma of writing on Khmer court music as a way of representing Cambodia, for example, when many Cambodians do not actively listen and participate in such traditions is obvious.

With such caveats in mind, and a flexible understanding of the terms, there are certain traditions, instruments, and ensembles that have come to be labeled by the local communities as classical. While I will address those traditions here the concept of classicization will be dealt with further in Chapters 4 and 5, as I discuss the forces of political activity and globalization on music.

Many significant traditions had their origins in royal courts, supported by kings and royal families. For some of these courtly traditions, particularly in Burma/Myanmar and Thailand, an audience outside of the royal palace was also significant. Many of the Thai, Burmese, and Khmer empires, furthermore, had periods of strength and periods of decline often with centuries before a new dynasty would arise. In the modern period, royal patronage of the arts was not always carried forth by the colonial (French, British) rulers or, in the case of Thailand, by a parliamentary system that replaced the absolute monarchy in the early 1930s. Vietnam's imperial court is long gone, and though its music survived until the 1970s, it was never widely known or played. Today it is revived as a regional symbol of the city of Hué and supported by a recording industry that packages it for tourists.

There are today in Thailand, Burma/Myanmar, and Cambodia fairly clear genres that have been dubbed "classical" by foreign researchers and by contemporary governments. While they are not always associated with the court (present or past) or with an elite audience they share some general traits. These include highly refined instruments in the lowlands, in contrast to predominantly vocal traditions and instruments of simple construction in the highlands; the cultivation of advanced technical skill, which may include extensive memorized repertoire and require long hours of practice; the professionalization of musicians (i.e., group of practitioners who won't necessarily have other means of livelihood); and a wide variety of ceremonial, ritual, or entertainment performance contexts.

MAJOR COURT ENSEMBLES

Before introducing specific ensembles of Burma/Myanmar, Thailand, Cambodia, and Vietnam I will give you a quick summary of some major trends found in many of the ensembles that you will listen to carefully in the discussion in this chapter.

One trend can be found in the choices of instruments (whether of complex or simple construction). Many of the ensembles in the region are dominated by wind and percussion instruments. The wind instrument is likely to be a reed-type aerophone (like an oboe, though often with more than two layers of reeds), and the percussion instruments often take the form of xylophones, gong chimes, and drum circles. While instruments made of a series of pitched gongs are common, there are not entire ensembles made up of gongs and xylophones. Gamelan ensembles—comprised largely of round gong or slab key idiophones though often including wind and string instruments—as found in Indonesia (see the volumes on Java and Bali in this Global Music Series), are not found in mainland Southeast Asia. In general, while gongs are found throughout the region they tend to recede into the background of the ensemble playing supporting parts and the double reed instrument takes a more prominent role. These are some of the marked differences between the mainland and the island traditions.

Because double-reed aerophones and percussion instruments are naturally quite loud, a rough distinction is made between ensembles that are generally found outdoors and used for festivals, celebrations, and theater, and those found indoors in a more intimate context. Lower volume indoor ensembles often include stringed instruments and often a flute substituting for the reed aerophone. This distinction between outdoor and indoor ensembles which prominently divided many traditions in the past has dissolved in recent years as amplification and other modern technologies have increasingly been adopted, allowing for different instrument groupings.

One further point pertinent to instruments has to do with their roles as part of an ensemble. The organization of instruments for much mainland Southeast Asian music often (again with a few notable exceptions) tends to assign one instrument per part. Instruments of the same type are not presented in mass sections, like the twenty violins of a symphony orchestra all playing together. Rather, instruments of contrasting timbre are found in the same ensemble, and it is usually clear which instrument is playing which part. Contrasting timbres and contrasting versions of the same melody reveal the nuances and idiosyncrasies of individual instruments and musicians. A heterogeneous sound (in contrast to a homogenous sound) is generally preferred, where distinctions in instrument timbre and also in performance style are clearly evident (see Wade 2009: 66).

In contrast to some of the more highly improvisatory traditions found to the west in India, much of the repertoire of mainland Southeast Asian music is made of predetermined pieces of set melodies and set forms. While predetermined, the performances of these pieces are not standardized. The bulk of these traditions are orally transmitted. Therefore, there is quite a bit of variation across different performances by different musicians. Furthermore, what constitutes the core "piece" of music is similarly somewhat flexible with different performances manifesting different melodic variations. Now I will turn to introducing you to some ensemble music that will give you the opportunity to listen for some of these specific characteristics. As I introduce ensembles, I'll introduce you to some additional musical trends.

Burma/Myanmar. The roots of traditional Burmese music can be found in the dynasties of the Burmese kings. Much of the court-derived music found in Burma today is thought to have been transmitted from the 133-year period of the last Konbaung dynasty (1752–1885). The Konbaung dynasty was quite supportive of the arts (some kings more than others), though much of that patronage ended with the takeover by the British. With this colonization Burma was officially annexed to and run as a province of India. This Konbaung dynasty, actually the third Burmese dynasty, was expansionist—with military campaigns into Manipur, Arakan, Assam, the Mon kingdom of Pegu in the South, and the Siamese kingdom of Ayutthaya—and its administrative center was always along the Irrawaddy river. One of the important ways that this military expansion influenced the court music was through the practice of bringing back musicians and artisans as spoils of war. When the Burmese sacked the Siamese capital of Ayutthaya in 1776, for instance, they returned to the palace on the Irrawaddy delta with thousands of artists and musicians as prisoners of war. Those prisoners were ultimately quite influential to the musical life of the country. I will return to this particular relationship in Chapter 5.

The ethnic concentration of the Burmese kingdoms was largely Burmese. The cultural power of the Burmese court had limited impact on the peripheries of the kingdom, as many of the hill tribes were not subject to its influence. Administrative, economic, and cultural influence (or power) diminished as one moved further from the capital or the palace. There is here a sharp contrast between the dominant Burmese make-up of the royal court and the contemporary demographics of the nation-state of Myanmar.

Two basic ensemble types were found in Burmese courts and can still be found today. The *saing waing* (*hsaiñwaiñ*) (literally "hanging circle"), or *saing*, takes its name from the method of hanging tuned drums on the inside of a circular frame to form the lead instrument of the ensemble. The *saing* is generally played out doors in loud, festival or ritual contexts. Indoor chamber music in contrast is used for intimate, quieter affairs and consists of a few or even one instrument with a singer (usually with bell and clapper). The indoor tradition does not have a specific name, as the instruments found in it are quite variable. Though the two ensemble types are used in different social contexts they share similar repertoire and theory (however the theoretical terminology is often quite different). Much of the repertoire has been preserved in collections of song texts called the *Maha Gita* (literally "great songs"). The melodies for the songs are passed down orally.

The Saing Waing Ensemble. The *saing waing* ensemble is the most commonly used outdoor ensemble (CD track 6, Figure 2.1). The *saing waing* consists of 6–10 players on membranophones, idiophones, and aerophones. The basic core of the ensemble consists of a drum circle (*patt waing*, literally "drum circle) (CD track 7), a gong circle (*kyi waing*, literally "copper/bronze circle"), and a reed aerophone (*hne*, pronounced with a slight nasalization at the beginning—like the English

FIGURE 2.1 *The saing waing ensemble, here played by a children's troupe at the national performing arts competition. Players visible from left to right—hne (seated, instrument held down), singer (standing), kyi waing, patt waing amd patt ma.*

word "hmm") (CD track 8). Additional instruments include a gong rack (*maung*), a large drum (*patt ma*), a set of side drums (*chauk lon batt*), a large bamboo clapper (*wa let kouke*), and a set of cymbals (*lingwin*).

The most common context for the Burmese saing waing is a *pwe*. The term *pwe* is used in Burma/Myanmar to refer broadly to a performative event such as a festival, performance, spirit propitiation ceremony (see vignette 1 in Chapter 1), ritual, theater, offering event, or party. Most *saing waing* troupes today make their living playing for various types of *pwe*. The selection on CD track 6 is performed by the Mandalay based saing waing troupe of Shwei Daung Myaing. At such an event the host of the *pwe* will hire a *saing waing* troupe (inclusive of singers and possibly comedians), set up a stage on the road in front of their home, and invite everyone in the neighborhood to attend. Even in urban Yangon/ Rangoon a *pwe* will block, traffic for the night, start around 7 or 8 in the evening, and go on until sunrise. Today, all instruments will be amplified through loudspeakers (often painfully loud) with lots of echo.

The uniquely Burmese drum circle (*patt waing*) consists of twenty-one tuned drums hung vertically by cords inside a circular frame that is elaborately decorated with gold paint and glass (Figure 2.2). Each

FIGURE 2.2   *Saing Waing troupe leader Sein Kyaw Naing setting up the patt waing.*

barrel-shaped drum has two heads, yet is only played on one end upon which a tuning paste, (*patt sa*, literally "drum food") is placed to tune the drums to a particular scale or mode. The tuning paste (traditionally made of rice and burnt tamarind but now made of a synthetic compound) is not permanently attached, but is removed completely at the end of a performance. Paste is added to or subtracted from particular drums to allow for different pitches, thus enabling the *patt waing* to be tuned to a different melodic mode. The *patt sa* allows the drums to be tuned precisely with bell-like tones of clear, exact pitch for playing melodies. Often during a performance the *patt waing* player will make minor tuning adjustments on the fly or during the solo of another instrument and may change the pitches of the drums significantly (see below). Similar use of tuned drums can be found in Thailand (in the *piphat mon* ensemble, but it has only seven tuned drums) and also in India called *tabla tarang*. Neither of these instruments are hung in a rack.

The *patt waing* player is the leader of the ensemble. The *saing waing* troupe will often take the name of the *patt waing* player, as in "the *saing waing* of Sein Kyaw Naing" (Figure 2.2). Though traditionally male, female *patt waing* players are increasingly found in the newer *saing waing* contexts such as national competitions and at the state universities (see Chapter 4). The *patt waing* player will hire (and fire) members, choose repertoire, secure gigs, and, of course, receive the most money. It is upon his reputation that a troupe is hired (or not).

Given its unmistakable timbre and its elaborate embellishment of melodies, the *hne* player (Figure 2.3) is often mistaken as the leader of the ensemble. The *hne* player will add to the heterophonic melodies with his/her own idiosyncratic version of the tune. Its unique sound quality has often led to a more prominent place in the engineered sound balance of some contemporary CDs—upsetting to many *patt waing* players who lead the ensembles. A third prominent instrument, the *kyi waing*, is a circle of tuned gongs that plays truncated versions of the melody. The different timbres of these three prominent instruments—a tuned drum that sounds like raindrops, a reed aerophone with a raspy shrill, and a bossed gong that sounds bell-like—combine to produce a small ensemble music quality to the ensemble in which each instrument can be distinguished. Other instruments such as large bamboo clappers (*wa let kouke*), a gong rack (*maung*), and a large bass drum (*patt ma*) fill out the sound. The heterogenous sound quality is an important part of the sound aesthetic.

ACTIVITY 2.2   *CD track 6 "Pabawin Tachin" is a song by the famous Saing leader Sein Be Da. It is here performed by the troupe of Shwei Daung Myaing.*

Listen to the example multiple times and notice the contrasting timbres of the instruments. Note the contrasts between by addressing the following:

Pick out and name all the instruments.

> Notice the relationship between the hne *and the* patt waing. *Draw a diagram that maps the contour of each? Are they playing the same melody?*
>
> Notice later the heterophonic relationship between the patt waing *and the voice.*
>
> *What other types of instruments do you hear?*

(a)

FIGURE 2.3a and b *The hne is made from a single piece of hardwood, bored with seven holes on the front and one for the thumb on the back. The reed is formed from toddy-palm leaf (after months of soaking and smoking) folded and cut to make six or eight layers creating a triple or quadruple double reed aerophone.*

(b)

FIGURE 2.3 *continued*

Burmese Modes and Tuning. Burmese music is based upon a seven-tone scale. Of those seven notes, five of them are primary and the remaining two are secondary. The orientation of the five primary notes determines the mode. The concept of mode is found throughout the world and refers to the pitch and melodic material on which composition and improvisation is based (see Chapter 4 of *Thinking Musically* (Wade 2009). In Burmese music a melody (in a particular mode) is made up largely of the principle five tones, with the other two notes used almost exclusively for ornamentation and embellishment. The same seven notes can be arranged into a different mode by rearranging which pitches are primary, which are secondary, and which one is the tonic or "home base." Figure 2.4 presents the four modes most commonly used by the *saing waing* ensemble. While there are seven theoretical modes, the remaining three are very rarely played (see Garfias 1975b). Western pitch terminology (C, D, E, etc.) is used by *patt waing* players though Western notation is not.

While there are other modes that the *saing waing* troupe will use, these are the most common. Notice in Figure 2.4 the relationship in pitch organization between one mode and another depicted by the Roman

Mode	Fundamental tones				
Than you hcau'pau	C	E	F	G	B
	I	III	IV	V	VII
Hkunithanci	G	B	C	D	F
	I	III	IV	V	VII
Pasabou	C	D	E	G	A
	I	II	III	V	VI
Ngapau	F	G	A	C	D
	I	II	III	V	VI

FIGURE 2.4 *The four most common modes used by the saing waing ensemble. Note the two most common mode types have the same basic arrangement (I II III V VI and I III IV V VII).*

numerals. The basic pentatonic (5 note) layout is found either as I III IV V VII (scale degrees 1 3 4 5 7) or as I II III V VI (scale degrees 1 2 3 5 6). Different modes have their tonic notes set at different pitches, giving similarly shaped modes slightly different moods.

In addition to the choice of basic pitches and the scale degree of the tonic, modes in Burmese music also have characteristic melodic ideas associated with them. A trained listener would be able to identify a particular mode from the particular melodic idioms that are always found in that mode.

ACTIVITY 2.3 *Using a keyboard or your voice, play or sing the pentatonic 5-note scale for the mode* than you hcau'pau *followed by* pasabou. *They both have the same tonic but they have a different selection of five notes.*

After familiarizing yourself with one or the other, improvise around the mode (moving up or down, repeating notes, etc.). Now intermittently add an embellishment of one of the secondary notes. Don't stay on the secondary note for long and never begin or end a musical phrase with a secondary note.

Listen again to CD track 6. Sing along with the voice that begins the piece. Listen for the tonic note (hint: the long phrases end on the tonic) and then sing around the pasabou *scale while listening.*

Listen a little more deeply to the sound of the patt waing. *How does its rendition of the melody differ from that of the* hne? *Can you hear the occasional secondary notes? Now listen closely to the voice. Notice the variations to the melody as presented through the voice.*

CD track 6 also has a vocal part. *Saing waing* performances would most always have a vocalist—in fact, the term used for *saing waing* without a singer or *pwe* context is *bala saing* (literally "naked *saing*"). Unlike much Western music, Burmese poetry avoids strong accents. The Burmese language is a tonal language. For the Burmese this means that there are four basic types of syllables: level, high and short, high and long, and glottal stops. Aficionados of Burmese poetry find aesthetic delight in the craft by which the artist rhymes lines both internal to a line of poetry and at the end of a line. With emphasis on rhyme, rather than rhythm, sung poetry tends to float above the rhythm of the accompanying instruments, often avoiding the strong accents of the ensemble.

In Burma/Myanmar the genre of a piece is largely dictated by its mode. The *Maha Gita* (the great book of songs) is organized around pieces in particular modes. The *saing waing* troupe will play pieces in several different modes throughout the course of an all night *pwe*. A single piece, however, usually stays in one particular tuning mode with occasional emphasis on other tonal centers within the piece. Contemporary composers that have been influenced by modulation or "changing keys" now compose pieces in more than one mode. However, for instruments such as the *patt waing* that require one to re-tune (add or subtract *patt sa*) such practice is difficult.

Burmese music is identifiable through its two-part pitch structure. Two distinct parts can be identified in this music. The *patt waing* player's right hand plays the upper melody while his (or increasingly her) left hand plays the supporting secondary part. This two-part arrangement will transfer to many other Burmese instruments. The gong circle (*kyi waing*), for example, often played by the apprentice to the *patt waing* player, consists of twenty-one small, bossed gongs on a circular frame. The physical arrangement of pitches is similar to that of the *patt waing* though it will not have the flexible tuning available to the *patt waing*. It plays material similar to that of the *patt waing* yet the rendition of a melody will be somewhat more skeletal. The *kyi waing* plays a heterophonic version of the melody that is less dense than that of the *patt waing*. Heterophony—one melody performed almost simultaneously and somewhat differently by multiple musicians (see Wade 2009: 131)—is common practice throughout mainland Southeast Asia. Learning how to listen to heterophonic textures is a key step to understanding and appreciating this music.

In addition to the distinct instruments, Burmese music is differentiated from other Southeast Asian musics through its use of a supporting melodic line. An instrument that can play the secondary part will always accompany singers, *hne* players, or other single pitch instruments. The *kyi waing* and the *patt waing*, unlike the *hne*, can play two notes at the same time. The secondary, supporting melody is lower in pitch and is a quickly identifiable feature in Burmese music that is not found in the music of Burma's/Myanmar's neighbors. The lower melody (generally played by the left hand on the *patt waing* and *kyi waing*) adheres strictly to the five tones of the mode being played. It is in the right hand melody where the secondary embellishment notes will be heard.

The diagram of *patt waing* tuning (Figure 2.5) should clarify the right hand distinction. The player sits in the middle of the circle. On his/her left are the lower tones played on the larger drums (look also at Figure 2.2 for comparison). The lower drums will be tuned to the five notes of a particular mode while the higher pitched drums on the right are tuned to all notes of the scale. For *pasabou* tuning (CD track 6) the 21 drums of the *patt waing* need to be tuned (from low to high) to pitches   5 6 1 2 3 5 6 1 2 3 5 6 7 1 2 3 4 5 6 7 1
in contrast to hkunithanci tuning 5 7 1 2 4 5 7 1 2 4 5 6 7 1 2 3 4 5 6 7 1
or than you hcou' pau tuning   5 7 1 3 4 5 7 1 2 3 5 6 7 1 2 3 4 5 6 7 1

Burmese Chamber Music. In contrast to the *saing waing* ensemble played with loud instruments such as the *hne*, the indoor chamber instruments have a much softer and more intimate sound. Stringed instruments are naturally much quieter and prior to the adoption of amplification could only be functionally played indoors. There is no specific name for the indoor ensembles but, rather, any of the quiet instruments (bamboo xylophone, harp, flute, slide guitar, piano, mandolin, etc.) would be categorized as indoor. These instruments could be played in an ensemble (though too many melody players is generally discouraged) or solo. As mentioned above, such distinctions have

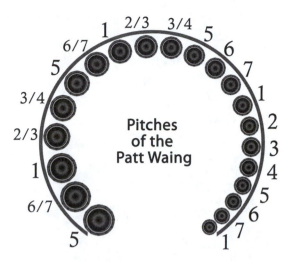

FIGURE 2.5   *Patt waing tunings.*

blurred in recent years with the adoption of microphones and studio technologies that can level the volume between instruments.

Common to both indoor and outdoor music and found in each ensemble type is the use of a set of rhythm instruments for articulating the basic rhythmic mode (see below) of the piece. For the *saing waing* ensemble larger, louder idiophones (cymbals and large clappers) mark out the time. For the indoor music, the hand-held *si* and *wa* (bell and clapper) are played to mark out time (Figure 2.6). The *si* consists of two bell-shaped cymbals attached by a string; it is held between the forefinger and thumb of the right hand. The bamboo *wa* is either made of two wooden shells pinched like castanets or of a piece of split bamboo; it is held in the left hand. The *si* and *wa* are often played by the singer.

The most prominent instrument of the indoor or chamber music tradition is the Burmese arched harp or *saung gauk*, (literally "harp arched") as shown in Figure 2.7 and heard on the CD track 9. The Burmese consider the *saung gauk*, or *saung*, to be their most prestigious instrument. The *saung* is revered as the national instrument of the country and is often (not unlike the piano in the West) found in the homes of citizens who may or may not play it. The standardized gold, red, and black design associates the instrument with the royal courts and with refined sophistication. Buddhist symbolism embedded in its construction also allows the player an intimate connection to both the court and the religious

FIGURE 2.6 *Si and Wa. Two sets of* si *(bell) and* wa *(bamboo clapper) are pictured.*

life of the Burmese. The extension of the neck beyond the strings is completely ornamental and ends in the figure of a stylized bodhi tree leaf. The bodhi tree, as mentioned in chapter 1, was the tree under which Buddha attained enlightenment. Players of the *saung* sit like the Buddha, under the bodhi leaf, while they play. Additionally, four holes are cut into the skin for aid in resonance. The holes, it is said, allow the *nat* spirits (recall vignette No. 3 from chapter 1) to come out and dance.

The harp is constructed from a hollowed-out piece of wood to which is attached a carved piece of wood (or more rarely the root) from the acacia tree (ideally the same wood from which the *hne* is made). The shape of the harp resembles that of a swan or a boat with an over-extended bow that rises up above the instrument. The 14–16 nylon or silk strings of the modern harp (18th and 19th century harps had fewer strings) stretch from the deer or goatskin-covered body to red silk chords and then are tied with a pinch knot onto the neck of the instrument. Many harp luthiers of late have opted for guitar-like tuners attached to the neck for easier tuning.

Harp players use a variety of tunings. The basic principles of the modal system employed by the *saung* players are similar to that of

FIGURE 2.7 Saung gauk (arched harp) *note the string tuning mechanism and bodhi tree icon at end of neck.*

the *saing waing,* though the terminology that each uses is distinct. The 7-tone scale has five primary tones and, as with the *saing waing,* mode is determined by the placement of the tonic pitch and by the relative arrangement of five primary pitches. On the *saung* the strings are generally tuned to the five primary pitches of the mode with the secondary notes achieved by pinching the string with the thumb of the left hand. The left hand—with some virtuosic exceptions—does not pluck the string. Melody is played by plucking with the first finger of the right hand while the secondary melodic line is played with the thumb of the right hand in much the same way that the parts were divided between right and left hand on the *patt waing.*

ACTIVITY 2.4 In Praise of the Burmese Harp *(CD track 9) is played by U Myint Maung in* hnyinlon *mode (roughly 1 3 4 5 7 with a fundamental on C). Hum or sing the mode first to get the rough feel for it in your head. Try and decipher*

> *the melodic line played by the first finger from the supporting line played by the thumb.*

As with melodic modes (determined by pitch selection and specific melodic ideas) there are recognized rhythmic modes articulated on the *si* and *wa*. All are organized in duple meter with the *wa* beat emphasizing the final beat in the cycle. The two most common rhythmic modes are *wa let si* and *na yi si*. *Wa let si*, the simplest rhythmic mode, is a two beat pattern alternating *si* and *wa* (if notated it would be scribed X O X O over 4 or 8 beats, where X = *si* and O = *wa*). *Na yi si* is a four beat pattern of two *si* beats, a rest, followed by a *wa* (X X – O). There are a variety of other rhythmic modes found articulated on the *si* and *wa*. On CD track 9 you can hear *na yi si* played by the singer Daw Yi Yi Thant. If you search for the full 12 minute recording of this piece, you'll hear the rhythmic mode change to *wa let si*.

Like many traditions in Southeast Asia, Burmese music places the accent on the final beat of the cycle. The *wa* clapper sound, ending the cycle, is the strong beat. You will also hear a significant slowing and delay of the *wa* beat, especially at the end of a verse of poetry. The last line of a stanza will be stretched out dramatically, pausing for a moment before a clap of the *wa* resolves the phrase.

ACTIVITY 2.5   *Listen again to CD track 9, this time focusing on famous Burmese singer Daw Yi Yi Thant. She is playing the* si *and* wa *at the same time that she is singing.*

Identify the rhythmic mode. Clap along with the si *and* wa *rhythm. Use right hand finger snaps for* si *beats and left hand slaps on your knee for* wa *beats. Feel for the phrase endings on the* wa *beats and the occasional pause just preceeding the* wa *clap at the end of a stanza.*

Notice the strict timing of the si *and* wa *simultaneously performed with an unaccented vocalization. It is almost as if the rhythm of the* si *and* wa *and the rhythm of her voice are unrelated. She completely avoids the strong accents.*

Another important instrument in Burmese chamber music is the bamboo xylophone or *pattala*, CD track 10. The *pattala* consists of twenty-four bamboo slats suspended (with an arching boat shape) over a resonating chamber of teak wood. Unlike the wooden xylophones (*ranāt*) of Thailand and Cambodia (see below) the bamboo *pattala* is not tuned with a tuning paste but rather the underside of each key is shaved to acquire the desired pitch: shaving the middle lowers the pitch; shaving the ends raises it (Figure 2.8). Compared to the tuning paste of the *patt waing* it is much more permanent.

FIGURE 2.8 *Tuning a pattala. In this picture, pattala maker U Tun Kyi has flipped the bars upside down to fine-tune it with a chisel.*

Historically, one of the primary contexts for the performance of Burmese chamber music would be in the home of a patron. A patron for a house concert would invite guests to his home for an evening of listening. Full appreciation of the nuances of the shifting modalities, the esoteric poetry, and the subtle styling of the vocals demands an audience of connoisseurs educated in the particularities of the tradition—no small feat. Such an audience is increasingly rare, and the economic conditions over the past forty years have, to make matters worse, permitted fewer and fewer patrons to hold lavish parties (where they would be expected to serve food). Today, these sounds are easily heard on Myanmar radio and television, at the state schools, and at national competitions, but house concerts are largely a context of the past.

Thailand and Cambodia. The court traditions of Thailand and Cambodia have much in common. Centuries of warfare, imperialism, and cultural and economic exchange between the Thai, Lao, and Khmer empires have resulted in strikingly similar court traditions of music and dance. Court support for the arts ended in Thailand with the 1932 military coup that ended the absolute monarchy. Similarly, 1970 saw the end of royal patronage in Cambodia when Marshal Lon Nol overthrew prince Norodom Sihanouk, leading to a period of great cultural devastation under Khmer Rouge rule. Today these musics are maintained primarily through the national educational system with government support essential to continuing the traditions in each country.

In commenting on the close similarities between Khmer and Thai culture—similar ensembles and instruments in their court music—some observers have been led to generalization about equivalence. Partially due to Thailand's economic success over the past century and its effective avoidance of colonialism, it is often assumed that the Siamese influence over Khmer culture is dominant. In fact, Khmer impact on Siamese traditions (and, importantly, the classical arts) is far deeper. Khmer culture was already well developed (and heavily influenced by Indic culture) by the 13th century when the Tai established their first kingdom in Sukhothai.

As noted above, the practice of capturing musicians, dancers, and artisans as spoils of war was common practice for many expansionist empires in the region. Just as the Burmese attacked the Thai capital of Ayutthaya and forcibly relocated Thai musicians to the Burmese palaces, multiple wars between the Siamese and the Khmer empires forced the migration of Khmer people to Siam, where the Siamese absorbed much from the Khmer: vocabulary, architecture, art, Buddhism, musical instruments, repertory, and dance. In a far different political situation years later, in the nineteenth and twentieth centuries, many Thai musicians, dancers, and composers were sent from the court in Bangkok to aid the Khmer in restoring their arts. This led to much of the apparent similarity in classical music and dance-drama (Sam, et al 1995: 159). Despite many surface similarities, however, the communities that define themselves as Thai or Khmer often perceive significant differences. "To a person with strong feelings about neighbors across the border, no difference is insignificant, and few Thai or Khmer easily forgive confusion on the issue" (Miller and Sam 1995:242).

Piphat (Thai), Pinn Peat (Khmer). The *piphat* (Figure 2.9, CD track 11) and the *pinn peat* (Figure 2.10, CD track 12) are the most revered and important ensembles in Thailand and Cambodia, respectively. Their primary functions are to serve important social events such as rituals and weddings where they perform the elite and refined compositions including court dance, masked plays, shadow plays, religious ceremonies, long narratives, and accompaniment to the Hindu Ramayana

FIGURE 2.9 *Piphat ensemble—Front row: ranat ek, ranat thum; Second Row: pi, khong wong, khong wong lek; third row: taphon, ching, klong that.* *(Photo courtesy of Pornprapit Phosavadi.)*

FIGURE 2.10   *Pinn peat ensemble—Front row: two singers, skor sampho, roneat ek, roneat thom, skor thom; Back row: kong tauch, sralai, kong tauch, chhing.*   *(Photo by Terry Miller.)*

(*Ramakien* in Thailand; *Reamker* in Cambodia). They also play alone. The *piphat* of the Mon people of Western Thailand (*piphat mon*) provides an ethnic variation on this ensemble. This particular ensemble, often played by Thai rather than Mon musicians, is used almost exclusively for funeral rituals (Wong 1998).

In both Thai and Khmer contexts there are multiple variations to the basic setup of the ensemble so that it ranges from five to thirteen instruments. Figure 2.11 lists instruments in the *piphat* and *pinn peat* ensemble with descriptions and rough equivalences of each. The full

Thai (Piphat)	Khmer (Pinn Peat)	Type
Pi nai	Sralai	Quadruple-reed aerophone
Ranat ek	Roneat ek	Higher-pitched xylophone
Ranat thum	Roneat thom or roneat thung	Lower-pitched xylophone
Khong wong yai	Kong thom	Lower-pitched gong circle
Khong wong lek	Kong tauch	Higher-pitched gong circle
Ching	Chhing	Small cup-shaped cymbals
Thon	Skor thaun	Goblet shaped single-headed drum
Taphon	Skor sampho	Horizontally-mounted barrel drum
Klong that	Skor thom	Pair of barrel drums
Klong kaek	Skor khek	Pair of long laced drums

FIGURE 2.11 *A comparison of Thai and Khmer instruments in the piphat and pinn peat ensemble edited from Miller and Sam's 1995 article "The Classical Musics of Cambodia and Thailand: A Study of Distinctions."*

list, found in Miller and Sam's useful article, "The Classical Musics of Cambodia and Thailand: A Study of Distinctions," consists of approximately twenty-five instruments that have different names but similar construction along with contextual similarities and differences.

The minimum instrumentation for the ensembles would include a reed aerophone, a xylophone, a gong circle, a pair of cymbals, a drum, and a vocalist.

The essential *piphat* ensemble (Figure 2.9), for example, consists of the higher-pitched xylophone *ranāt ēk*, the lower-pitched circular gong-chime *khong wong yai* (Figure 2.12), *pī* (the quadruple-reed aerophone that gives its name to the ensemble) plus *ching* (a pair of small cymbals) and one or two drums: *taphōn, klong song nā,* or *klong khaek*.

Despite the similarities in instruments and playing contexts there are notable differences in the performance practice, leadership, organization and interpretation between the Thai and Khmer ensembles. Both traditions draw from a repertoire of orally transmitted melodies, which find subtle variation across each instrument in the ensemble. However, the Thai conceive of the lower-gong circle (*khong wong yai*) as representing the most fundamental form of the melody while in the Khmer tradition

FIGURE 2.12   *Khong wong yai, Thai gong circle.*   *(Photo by Don Traut.)*

the voice holds the purest form of the melody. If there is no vocal part the Khmer think of the reed (*sralai*) as carrying the melody. For Khmer court music in general, instruments like the flute, reed aerophone, and bowed lute that imitate the voice are therefore the instruments to focus on to find the melodic "ground." As each instrument develops slight variations from the basic melody, it is important to know where to focus your listening in order to find the most basic version of the melody.

ACTIVITY 2.6   *Listen to CD track 11 and pick out each of the instruments.*

Do the same for CD track 12.

Would you say that the ensemble sound texture in each case is homogeneous or heterogeneous?

While listening, play along with the ching/chhing *player. Notice the occasional change of rhythmic density. Notice the rhythmic relationship between your* ching/chhing *part and the other instruments.*

Pleng Homrong Kleun Kratob Fang (Sounds of the Surf Overture)

Listening Guide for CD track 11

00:00	Solo *pi*, free rhythm
00:27	entrance of the *ching*, followed by *taphon* (approx 30 bpm) and ranat
00:47	antiphonal passages back and for the between *pi* and *ranat*, and *khong wong yai*. Each plays slightly different verision of the melody. Ascending and descending melody on *pi* and *ranat* are echoed by the *khong wong yai*
1:45	spliting the melody half *pi/ranat*, second half *khong wong yai*
2:23	all together
2:37	new melody
	notice the density of the the *pi* in relation to the *khong wong yai* and both in relation to the *ching*
3:08	new melody (based on previous) alternated between *pi* and *kong wong yai*. *Ranat* continues to play throughout
4:20	half phrases
4:30	quarter phrases
4:39	all playing together
5:00	a third melody alternating between *pi* and *khong wong yai*
5:44	shorter phrases
5:53	all together

Roeung Supheak Leak (The Story of Supheak Leak). An example of roeung, narrative dance, performed by the Sam-Ang Sam ensemble.

Listening Guide for CD track 12

0:00	all instruments playing intro on roneat
	chhing and *sampho* on steady pulse beat (approx 160 bpm)
	sralai lead instrument
	kong thom playing slightly truncated version of the melody

1:49	stretched out cadence
2:08	new melody
	slightly slower
	chhing tempo cut in half (approx 72 bpm)
4:17	voices enter
	chhing tempo cut in half again (approx 24 bpm)

Totuol damrah	Receiving the order
Preah phouvaneat	of your highness,
bangkum tror bat	I salute at your feet,
preah chao chaom mkott	oh crowned king,
prasoeur phott thlai euy	great one,
sdech yeang teou	as you depart

5:35	return of full ensemble
5:39	*chhing* returns to fast tempo (bpm 160)

Melody in both the Thai and Khmer traditions is regulated by cyclic patterns articulated on the drum and small cymbals (*ching*, Thai; *chhing* Khmer). The core patterns heard most clearly for both traditions on the small cymbals are based on a four-beat cycle, alternating "ching" strokes (open, ringing) with "chap" strokes (closed, damped). The basic (ching, chap, ching, chap; o + o +) pattern is found at different levels of density within a piece. The *ching/chhing* cyclic pattern is paralleled by a cyclic drumming pattern. A phrase at the first level lasts four measures, second-level eight, and a third-level phrase lasts sixteen. Varying degrees of melodic ornamentation will fill out the phrase depending on the density level of the pattern. The Thai system is far more extensive and nuanced than the Khmer but a basic four-beat structure (articulated at various levels of density) prevails. As in the Burmese traditions the final stroke of the cycle is the focal point of the cycle.

The Thai language is tonal and the Khmer is not. A tonal language is a language that uses tone and tone contour to distinguish words. Thai, for example, has five distinct tones: low, mid, rising, high, and falling. The same syllable pronounced with a different tone would create a different word. Tonal languages are found throughout Asia, including Burmese, Thai, Vietnamese, and Mandarin. The differences that this imposes in the creation of a melody are, of course, lost to those who do not speak Thai (tonal) or Khmer (non-tonal). However, the distinction triggers totally different procedures in generating melody in relation to text (Miller and Sam: 234). The Thai singer constructs the vocal version based on a skeletal outline of the melody (as most basically heard on the *khong wong yai*) yet must manage the contour of inflection to realize each syllable of text based upon its necessary tonal inflection. In contrast, the Khmer singer—singing the purest form of the melody—is not confined by linguistic tone rules.

Perhaps the most notable distinction between Thai and Khmer playing styles is the tendency for Khmer musicians to not only play somewhat slower (often with less virtuosity) but to perform melodies with a long-short rhythmic lilt in contrast to the steady consistent rhythm of a Thai performance. While this trait most clearly distinguishes Khmer from Thai music it is, of course, not consistent throughout either country. Sam-Ang Sam, a leading figure in the preservation of Khmer arts, notes that "as one moves westward toward Thailand, this rhythmic feature becomes less and less pronounced; musicians from Siem Reap [to the west], for example, play nearly even rhythms" (Sam, et al. 1995: 182).

ACTIVITY 2.7 *Listen to the* piphat *ensemble play* Pleng Homrong Kleun Kratob Fang, *(Sounds of the Surf Overture, CD track 11) and the* pinn peat *ensemble play* Roeung Supheak Leak *(Supheak Leak Dance Drama, CD track 12) back to back.*

Clap along with the ching and chap strokes emphasizing the final beat in the cycle.

Once you are comfortable with the ching and chap strokes, listen to the drums. Do you hear patterns?

Can you identify the slightly different approach to rhythm: a slight long-short lilt in the Khmer and a steadier pattern in the Thai?

What similarities do you notice in the two musical selections, in the melody, the rhythm, and the texture?

Find a video performance of each of these traditions online. What other similarities and differences can you find?

Both Thai and Khmer society is, even today, deeply gendered. While challenged in some contemporary contexts the performers of *piphat* and *pinn peat* music are predominantly male. Men traditionally play the core instruments of the ensemble—the gong circle, the xylophone, and the reed instruments and drums—and women generally play stringed instruments or sing. Such gendering is reinforced, with only occasional exception, in national music schools where boys gravitate to the *piphat* and *pinn peat* instruments. While the *piphat* and *pinn peat* share many performance contexts and social meanings (rituals, court dance, masked plays, shadow plays, religious ceremonies), some events in which one finds *pinn peat* and *piphat* ensembles are uniquely Thai or Khmer.

Wai Khru.   One of the most important rituals for all Thai musicians is the *wai khru* ceremony of paying homage to the teacher (*khru* from the Indian *guru*). In this ceremony music considered to be the most important and of the highest status will be played. This ceremony is of fundamental importance in Thai music culture. Thai classical musicians must be initiated through a series of rituals before altars bearing masks of deified Hindu and Buddhist figures from Indian religious literature. Through this ritual, musicians (and many other artists such as boxers, dancers, and singers who have similar ceremonies), establish a relationship through their teachers, to their teachers' teachers, and to the Hindu-Buddhist deities and cosmology that underpin the arts. In a ceremony that lasts several hours a *piphat* ensemble performs highly revered compositions in alternation with a ritualist, who chants auspicious texts in the Pali language. The students in this ritual also are led through recitations of Buddhist scripture in Pali language. The ceremony links the *piphat* ensemble to the students, the students to their teacher's lineage and the tradition's relationship to royalty and religion is reaffirmed (See Myers Moro 1988:319–327, and Wong 2001). The *piphat* ensemble, like many ritual ensembles, guides the progression of the ceremony, providing entry to an alternate state of mind. The overture (*homrong*) to the *wai khru* is an "ephemeral doorway through which deities can come and go, it is a frame of sound that *is* the sacred in action. Without this frame, deities could not be present and ritual events would not be sacred" (Wong and Lysloff 1991: 339).

Apsara Dance.   One of the most important roles of the *pinn peat* ensemble in Cambodia is to accompany *apsara* an indigenous dance. *Apsaras* are female dancers or heavenly maidens found in Hindu mythology who link the earthly kingdom to the world of the gods. Images of these *apsara* celetial nymphs can be found in the stone reliefs of Angkor Wat.

The contemporary *apsara* dance tradition draws from these Angkorian images implying (at least symbolically) an unbroken tradition of court dance stretching back to the monarchs of Angkor (see Figure 1.6 and 1.7). Despite its Hindu connections, *apsara* is regarded as quintessentially Khmer, regarded as the national dance, revived at the national arts schools, found in all tourist shows throughout the country, and a major cultural heritage activity among overseas Cambodian communities. Khmer dance and music scholar Amy Catlin has made several wonderful films (see additional resources) that supplement much of this material.

Other Thai and Khmer Ensembles. Other major ensembles in these two traditions also share similar instruments and contexts. The *mahori/ mohori* (Thai/Khmer) ensemble of both Thailand and Cambodia does not preside over important civic and religious rituals. It is light in character and is used in secular contexts and, more recently, to accompany plays and folkdances. It serves a purpose more in the role of entertainment and accompanying of certain dance traditions primarily to entertain guests at banquets. While there are, again, multiple variations of instrumentation in these ensembles the essential difference is the use of flute and stringed instruments (bowed and plucked). The *saw sam sai*, a three-string bowed lute is, historically, the leader of the Thai *mahori* while the Khmer ensemble does not include the three-stringed bowed lute but does include other two-stringed bowed lutes. The instrumentation often varies depending on ownership, patronage, and availability— today the *saw sam sai*, despite its historical prominence, is often omitted in Thai *mahori*. In Thailand, a third major ensemble type, *kruang sai* (string ensemble), heard on CD track 13, is of fairly recent (20th century) origin (Figure 2.13). It does not have an equivalent in Cambodia.

While any experienced musician of either tradition can instantly distinguish Khmer music from Thai music, for many outsiders discerning the difference depends on years of experience. While local and national interpretations of Thai-ness or Khmer-ness, of purity and origin, can be debated at length, we see here evidence of hundreds of years of cultural exchange between these two groups. Similar terminology, instruments, performance contexts, and performance practice reflect larger cultural patterns that help us understand the classical music in this area. Other cultural similarities—Theravada Buddhism, agriculture, geography, etc.—can reinforce these musical cultural trends. In contrast, however, we also can see hundreds of years' worth of local interpretation whereby a group (or a nation) makes a tradition its own, reinforcing and emphasizing difference to assert cultural uniqueness.

FIGURE 2.13 *Thai Kruang Sai ensemble. Instruments from left to right at back are saw u (two stringed bowed lute with coconut shell body), ching, khlui (flute) [hidden], thon (right hand goblet drum), rammana (left hand drum), saw duang (two stringed bowed lute with wooden body); front jakhe (plucked zither). Note the gender roles.* (Photo by Don Traut.)

Today the court musics of Thailand, Cambodia, and Burma/Myanmar have largely become the iconic musics of the state and they are the traditions most patronized by state sponsored educational facilities. But this contrasts somewhat with the situation in Vietnam.

Vietnam.   While scholars generally agree, with some debate, what styles and genres fit the "classical" category in Burma/Myanmar, Thailand, and Cambodia the court music of Vietnam has not found the same status. Indeed, the label "Vietnamese classical music" has no clear meaning. The music of Vietnam's imperial court survived until shortly after WWII but it was never widely known or played. Today, it has been revived in Hue, but tends to represent that ancient capital more than the nation as a whole. For these reasons Vietnamese music is often referred to as "traditional" rather than classical or court.

The population of Vietnam (approximately 85 million) can be divided into the Việt or lowland (largely urban) and the 53 upland minority groups. In Vietnamese contexts it is much more difficult to draw a line between the music of the political and economic elite and the music of the folk and ethnic minorities. Vietnam's long and narrow geography and its great regional variation resist generalizations across the entire country. The old way of thinking of Vietnam as divided into three (north, central, and south) general areas has been complicated by the division of the country into North and South during the 1950s and by increased media distribution of styles, growth of popular music traditions, internal migration and, more recently, an increased role of the national government in the arts.

Vietnamese traditional music is, for the most part, played on instruments derived from China, a result of close to one thousand years of occupation. However, Vietnamese modifications and local interpretations—sculpted to fit Vietnamese aesthetics—make this music significantly different from the traditional music of China. Perhaps the most conspicuous aspect of Vietnamese music is its degree of melodic ornateness, most obvious on the prominent chordophones. The modal system found in Vietnamese music largely depends upon specific ornaments or vibrato that articulate certain tones.

Vietnamese Instruments. Stringed instruments (*dàn*) heard on CD tracks 14 and 15, are prominent in Vietnam and are the instruments most identified with the Vietnamese traditions. String vibrations, slides, and bends and a wide variety of ornamentation are reflective of the vocal idiosyncracies and nuances. They point to the close connection between melody and the tonal Vietnamese language. Several Vietnamese *dàn* stand out.

Đàn Bầu (monochord). This uniquely Vietnamese instrument can be traced back to 7th century northern Vietnam (Figure 2.14). The player holds a bamboo pick in the right hand and plucks the steel string at the 1/2, 1/3, 1/4, etc. points on the string to produce a bell-like tone called a harmonic. To embellish notes and to change the string tension and, thus, allow different harmonics, the left hand moves a flexible handle carved from bamboo or buffalo horn and attached to a gourd (*bầu*) (CD Track 14).

ACTIVITY 2.8 *Listen to Phong Nguyen playing a dán bầu on CD track 14. Notice the clean, bell-like timbre of the tones. Notice also the embellishments, the bends and curves, placed on the notes as they are ringing.*

Find a guitarist who can show you how to play a harmonic on a guitar string. If you can find an electric guitarist whose guitar has a tremolo arm (or "whammy bar") have him/her show you how to manipulate the tension of the string with the tremolo arm while a note or harmonic is ringing.

The *đán bàu* can be found in multiple contexts: played solo or accompanying folk songs. It has been both an instrument of blind street musicians and the premier instrument of choice of the Tran imperial court (1225–1400) (Nguyen 1995: 471). The diversity of social contexts in which it has been found over the centuries provides a clear example of the inseparability of classical/court/folk categories when discussion Vietnam.

FIGURE 2.14   *Đàn Bàu, Vietnamese monochord.*   (*Photo courtesy of Phong Nguyen.*)

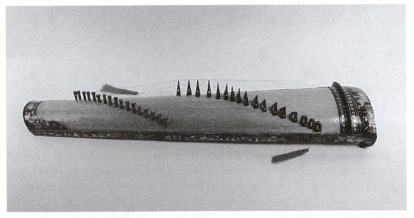

FIGURE 2.15 *Đàn tranh, the 16 or 17-stringed Vietnamese zither.* *(Photo courtesy of UW ethnomusicology archives.)*

Đàn Tranh (zither).   The *đàn tranh,* seen in Figure 2.15, is a 16 or 17 stringed board zither of paulownia wood. It is a Vietnamese adaptation of the Chinese *guzheng* and a relative of other East Asian board zithers such as the Korean *kayagum* and the Japanese *koto.* Though the repertoire and theory of the *đàn tranh* remains distinct from these other East Asian zithers, the similar construction and design is clear, again showing strong Chinese influence in contrast with the stronger Indic influence found throughout the rest of the mainland. The *đàn tranh* was used in court music before the 1800s and is presently popular in chamber ensembles, particularly in the central and southern areas. Tuned pentatonically, the strings are strung loosely over tall moveable bridges behind which the left hand may press to achieve additional notes (allowing for 6 and 7 note scales) as well as the characteristically Vietnamese bends and slurs between pitches (CD track 15).

ACTIVITY 2.9 *Compare and contrast Vietnamese and Chinese music for zither.*

Vietnamese musicians modified Chinese-derived instruments with high frets, looser strings, and a different style of decoration. While many dismiss Vietnamese instruments as simply Chinese, the approach to melodies and pitches involves a

different approach—one that is impossible to realize on Chinese instruments.
Look for photo, audio, and video examples of Chinese zithers. In particular examine the Chinese qin *and the* guzheng. *Which of these is closely related to the Vietnamese* đàn tranh? *Explain your rationale. What are some noticeable differences?*

Other notable Vietnamese string instruments also have the capacity for bent or sliding notes due to their loose strings or high bridges. Among many others these include *đàn nhị*, a two string fiddle similar to the Chinese *erhu* and the Thai *saw duang*, and the *đàn nguyệt*, a two string 8–12 fret, long-necked lute (also called the moon lute).

The contexts for Vietnamese traditional music are many and varied. These instruments can be found in a multitude of formal and informal, sacred and secular settings. Theatrical traditions abound in Vietnam, from the famous water puppet theater to classical theater with many regional variations. They provide an important context for many of these instruments. One of the most significant music theater traditions of the 20th century is the reformed opera known as *cải lương*. I will discuss *cải lương* further in chapter 5. For a preview listen to CD track 16 and note the similarities in sound to CD track 14 and 15.

CONCLUSION

While the terms "classical" and "court" are somewhat problematic in mainland Southeast Asia there are certain instruments and ensembles— most notably in Burma/Myanmar, Thailand, and Cambodia—that do have association with a past aristocracy, with elite patronage, or with an aesthetic of refinement. I will now move to discuss traditions that, while equally important to the region, do not have the same access to elite patronage. Focusing on some of the many different ethnic communities living in the region highlights explicitly the diversity of the region and will also set the stage for our later themes of political struggle and globalization. Minority and folk traditions, often enjoyed by a larger percentage of the population and sometimes interacting with the traditional or court musics, are equally important to understanding musics in each of these countries.

CHAPTER 3

Diversity and Regional Variation

THE CONCEPT OF ETHNICITY IN SOUTHEAST ASIA

In mainland Southeast Asia there are over two hundred named ethnic groups. Many of these groups are referred to by more than one name, and even the manner by which an ethnic group is determined varies considerably from place to place. How do we begin to study such a confusing situation? The cultural diversity found in this area of the world has forced scholars (largely anthropologists and historians) to confront the very concept of ethnicity with a critical eye. They have raised questions such as these: How does one determine one's ethnicity? To what traits does one appeal? Is ethnicity rooted in blood relations or in social relations?

ACTIVITY 3.1 *What is your ethnicity? To what traits do you appeal when you refer to that ethnicity (genetic heritage, customs, etc.)? Do you share the same ethnicity with all four of your grandparents? If not, in what ways are you different—do you identify with one grandparent more than another?*

In what way does your behavior portray your ethnicity (music, food, clothing, or otherwise)?

How does the expression of your ethnicity (in your behavior) differ from that of your parents or your grandparents?

Is it possible to change your ethnicity?

Discuss these questions with your classmates. Do you have similar or different conceptions of what comprises ethnicity?

A major challenge to the scholarly concept of ethnicity and tribal identification came from research in this area by Edmund R. Leach in his 1954 work, *Political Systems of Highland Burma*. Leach had set out before WWII to study a "tribe"—the Kachin, living in upper Burma—through fieldwork in what he thought was a representative community of this tribe. His research was complicated when he traveled throughout the Kachin hills visiting other Kachin villages. He came to realize that, contrary to dominant Anglo-American anthropological conventions, the Kachin were not a people with a single language, a common social structure, and an unchanging political system (1954, 281). Rather, the Kachin included speakers of several distinct languages (Jingpaw, Maru, Nung, and Lisu), had a social structure that oscillated between two different types through time, and were organized politically in relationship to another quite different people, the Shan (see Keyes 2002: 1170). Leach's work foreshadowed the development of theories of ethnicity that emphasize the interactions between peoples rather than their essential differences. The concept of ethnicity by this understanding is dependent more on relationships between groups (often political or economic) than it is on specific traits (language, skin color, etc.)

The differences among Southeast Asian communities must, from this perspective, be examined in relation to other groups in the area. Ethnicity must be viewed as a continuing process. It is relational rather than essential and is constantly changing. As relationships change, so will the sense of self and community. Often, or even usually, people do not have a single sense of "identity" but multiple ones as they relate to different groups of people. What is important in this anthropological definition is the notion that ethnicity is determined vis-à-vis another group of people. Without another group there is no ethnicity. Ethnicity then is something to be constantly negotiated to maneuver around the realities of group politics. The student of ethnicity must recognize that identity is not static and that human behavior and group allegiance, though historically informed, is constantly changing. As behavior that articulates group identity, music, dance, and theater are prime conduits through which to study ethnicity.

I will begin my explorations of ethnic diversity by discussing some of the multiple ways that ethnicity can be understood in the region. Some ways of defining ethnicity (e.g., language) contrast and overlap with other ways of defining it (e.g., religion). Some categories may be more prominent at some times, or more peripheral in different localities. Contemporary forces play into the formation and destruction of ethnic identity. Defining a group through its language might be complicated by the practice of multilingualism or by state language policies; identity defined by a particular location might be challenged by the flow of people from one area to another; nationalizing forces of homogenization are challenged by an assertion of the local; tourist sites and refugee camps are additional spaces that may also challenge a sense of identity.

The boundaries that demarcate the countries of Southeast Asia are largely colonial inventions of the past two centuries. Through a process of nationalizing in most countries, regional and largely mono-ethnic communities have come to dominate the political and economic arenas (Tai in Thailand, Khmer in Cambodia). In many cases the musical traditions, symbols, and discourses of the dominant groups come to represent the nation to the international community. Speaking musically, this has often led to the illusion that Thai music is representative of Thailand, or Khmer music representative of Cambodia. This provides a somewhat distorted picture, for numerous ethnic groups in all of these countries engage in radically contrasting traditions to that of the mainstream. Even within the dominant ethnic groups of each country the music often chosen by the elite or the state as emblematic of the nation, say the music found at state functions or in the national schools, does not necessarily reflect the musical preferences and practices of the majority of the people. Folk or popular traditions may be more representative of the dominant ethnic group than the musics heard in the schools or on the national stages. This contradiction, however, is by no means unique to mainland Southeast Asia. Is the music found in most American music schools representative of the United States?

Language Families. Because many of the minority communities span across political borders and, as such, cannot be differentiated by country, many scholars instead have organized the cultural diversity in Southeast Asia by language family with four principle families found. Language however, if we remember from Leach above, is not always a stable trait of cultural identity—particularly in an area where people may be fluent in several at a time. It is, thus, one of many unstable trait categories. Figure 3.1 maps the following language families.

Sino-Tibetan: Many minority languages from India, Western China, and Myanmar such as Burmese, Naga, Karen, Chin

Austroasiatic: Includes the majority Khmer of Cambodia and the Mon of Southern Burma and Southwest Thailand as well as Viet Muong in Vietnam and Laos

Tai: Mainstream majority of Thailand and Laos, Shan of Burma, Lao, Yay, Nùng, Khün

Austronesian: Cham of lowland Vietnam and Cambodia, Malay

It must be kept in mind that many people in this area of the world speak multiple languages. One language may be spoken at home, another in government offices of schools, another in the weekly market, still another to communicate with a neighboring group with whom they might trade. Furthermore, plenty of locals can sing along, in a limited way, with the latest pop hits from Japan, China, India, and the U.S. While some of these languages have millions of speakers, others are endangered and may have fewer than 5,000 speakers.

> **ACTIVITY 3.2**   *Search the Internet to find sites that discuss many of the ethnic minorities found in mainland Southeast Asia. Make a list of different ethnic groups. Here are a few groups to get you started: Karen, Shan, Chin, Kachin, Wa, Rohingya, Akha, Intha, Danu, Pa-O, Padaung, Mon, Karenni, Naga, S'gaw, Lao, Lisu, Lahu, Katu, Khorat, Dai, Cham, Yao, Cham, Tampuan, Hoa, Montagnard, Malay. There are many others.*
>
> *Return to your blank map (from Activity 1.2) and put them in.*
>
> *Which groups are the largest? Which groups cross over national borders?*
>
> *Can you tell which groups seem to dwell mostly in an upland area? Is there any evidence of a particular lifestyle (clothing, food, living patterns, etc.) that is revealed in their online presentation? Who is presenting the information (A member of the group? A tourist agency? A government? An aid organization?) What are their priorities in presenting this information?*

You hopefully noticed from Activity 3.2 that many of these groups live away from the river deltas in the highland regions. Lowland and highland is another rough duality through which anthropologists, political scientists and musicologistists have organized groups of people in Southeast Asia. These categories have been very useful for

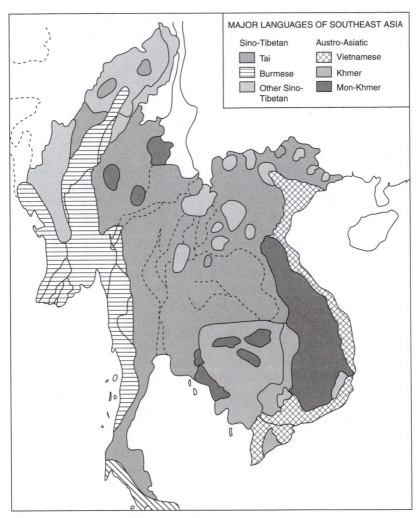

FIGURE 3.1   *Major language families of mainland Southeast Asia.*

73

understanding different social relationships, economic patterns, and agricultural practices. All of the countries under discussion have both lowland plains that are drained by major rivers (review Activity 1.2) and upland areas that are comparatively remote with fewer roads and rough terrain. The major cities lie in the lowlands, often on the deltas, where they have been home to the Hindu-Buddhist royal courts and remain the centers of political power today. The lowland plains host huge wetland rice farming areas that can support the wealth of royalty, an army, and large populations. These cities have been the commercial and administrative centers of the region.

The uplands in contrast, with expansive plateaus, rugged mountain ranges, and dense jungles house fewer people. The often-rugged terrain and higher elevation force distinct farming and sustenance practices such as hunting and gathering and shifting swidden (slash and burn) agriculture. The practice of shifting agriculture has historically meant that many of these communities would move around regularly—though this has become increasingly difficult in modern times.

Over the centuries people have migrated back and forth between upland and lowland areas. People would migrate (not always voluntarily) to the urban areas or to the valleys for economic or other benefit. Conversely, people would escape the reach of administrative control and remove to the hills where they would enjoy greater political autonomy. Such flow of people has increased significantly as the infrastructure (roads, electricity, etc.) extend further into the rural areas. These changes have made the distinct lifestyles and practices between lowland and upland communities increasingly ambiguous. The economic expansion of major cities, particularly through the late 20th century, increased the exchange of culture between people in the peripheries and people closer to the seats of power.

Continuing to the present, migrant laborers from the upland areas have consistently been drawn to the cities for economic opportunity. Workers throughout Asia's major cities migrate from the villages to the cities and often send money back to support the village. This economic relationship between villages and large cities continues through today. Cities, with their diverse mix of people, offer more cultural (and musical) diversity than the countryside and, while many pockets of major cities find people living in dire poverty, the economic wealth generally tends to locate in urban areas. The comparative poverty of the village (less so perhaps in areas of Thailand but dire in some regions of Burma and Cambodia) may in some cases contribute to the preservation of traditional lifestyles. Limited access to education, transportation, and the national and international media networks mitigate the exchange of musical ideas.

Because many ethnic groups span borders, the relationship between ethnic identity and national identity further complicates our quest to understand ethnic identity in mainland Southeast Asia. Contemporary nation-states spend a great deal of resources cultivating devotion and loyalty to one's own country—a topic I shall return to in the next chapter. These state-encouraged trends toward nationalism are often perceived as homogenizing forces in which dominant communities (or ethnicities) tend to overpower other voices. Reactions to such processes often end in assimilation and adoption by smaller groups of the cultural patterns of the dominant group. In other cases they provoke ethnic or regional reactionary movements that contribute to a variety of countercultural performance types or even armed resistance. For example: the Karen in Myanmar fight to maintain a distinct, non-Burmese, identity, as do many Isan Laotians in Thailand or Montagnards in Vietnam. Such cultural politics often work against national projects that seek to unify and consolidate the arts such as schools and museums.

Identifying ethnicity can be examined as a national projection, a concept informed by the politics of nation building. Vietnam and Thailand and more recently Myanmar have each sponsored ethnological research to determine the distinguishing characteristics of peoples living in the uplands. Unlike a linguistic approach, all of these research projects have been predicated on an assumption that differences can be determined *scientifically*, i.e., through a process of measuring features. The role of the national governments in measuring, determining and labeling ethnic groups (based on their criteria) cannot be underestimated in the region. Put to different uses some states actively homogenize or normalize their different communities, some are ambivalent and some embrace the cultural diversity. The role of the state in organizing, determining, projecting, and authenticating ethnicity must be kept in mind. States have bound together but also separated groups of people. In some cases states have pursued cultural integration, in others not at all, in still others it has been actively opposed. The reactions by the ethnicities to such state interventions is sometime in agreement with the state, but often in opposition to it.

ACTIVITY 3.3   *Visit the websites for the governments of each of these countries (Myanmar, Thailand, Cambodia, and Vietnam)*

How are ethnic minorities discussed and represented?
What images are used to portray these minorities? What type
of language is used? What type of clothing? What evidence of
pride or marginalization in these groups (minorities, races, tribes)
can you assess? Is there any reference to music, dance, or other
expressive arts in their discussions of minorities?

You will note from the websites of certain countries that ethnic minorities are often quite visible, at least as a token. The governments of both Vietnam and Myanmar claim that they have the most diverse populations in the area and actually quantify the number of distinct ethnicities in the country at 54 and 135 respectively. The criteria for differentiating one group from another is, however, not always clear.

Two other contemporary spaces have presented challenges to understanding concepts of ethnicity and cultural identity; these are the refugee camp and tourist spaces. Refugee camps are complicated non-state spaces where groups of people, often minorities from neighboring countries, live in relative isolation. With well over 100,000 people living in various camps in mainland Southeast Asia—some for over thirty years—refugee camps have become places that demand attention (see Reyes-Schramm 1999). In contrast, the growing tourist industry (especially in Thailand, but quickly growing in Vietnam) provides opportunities to stage and manufacture particular images of cultural diversity often historically contrived. In addition to being places with an influx of foreign ideas, tourism encourages the presentation and packaging of cultural images for consumption. How different groups are represented and who is in control of that representation, becomes an important question to understanding these people.

Musical Differences Between Groups. In many cases the minority musics of Southeast Asia, at least prior to recent changes brought on by quickly expanding media access, have been so radically different from the dominant court/classical traditions that few musical parallels can be made. Studying the formal organization of the Burmese *saing*, the Thai *piphat* or the Khmer *pinn peat*, will not necessarily help in understanding the minority traditions of Burma/Myanmar, Thailand, and Cambodia.

One important distinction that can be made between many ethnic minority traditions and the musics drawn from the lowland court traditions is in the societal role of the musician. The support given to

musicians through courts and the aristocracy as well as formal insti-
tutionalized rituals has developed a professional class of musicians in
many of the lowland areas that is not found in the highlands. People
who are required to work year-round to maintain the house and family
tend not to be exclusively musicians. Such professionalization in the
lowlands often leads to very different criteria for evaluating the quality of a performance, based on structural and performative aspects
of the sound—in contrast to quality being determined by sociological
factors. This, however, does not imply that the musics of the upland or
rural areas are any less difficult, complex or aesthetically developed.

It would be near impossible to productively generalize across the
region about the character of minority musical traditions at large.
Several contrasting case studies, of the hundreds possible, will serve to
elucidate some of the cultural diversity in the region.

ETHNIC DIVERSITY IN BURMA/MYANMAR

Shan state in northeast Burma/Myanmar—bordering China, Laos,
and Thailand—is the largest state in the country and consists largely of
rural highlands with only three modestly populated cities—Kengtung,
Lashio, and Taunggyi. The majority Shan population speaks a Tai language and has much in common culturally with its Thai neighbors to
the east. Few roads cover the area, though the northern road to Lashio
has regular traffic trucking goods to and from China. The markets of
Lashio, the last major city before the border, are filled with goods from
China and many of the inhabitants of the city are involved with Chinese
trade. Fears circulate around the country about how strong the economic presence of China is and how dominant the Chinese influence
has become over the past few decades.

Further south, the state capital, Taunggyi ("Great Mountain"), is
home to a diverse population of approximately 200,000. Situated to the
southeast of Mandalay (and close to 4500 ft. higher), Taunggyi provides
a respite from the heat of the Irrawaddy river valley and the dust of
Mandalay. The upland regions of Southeast Asia can actually get quite
cold, and the pine forests of the Shan plateau break the stereotype of hot,
humid Southeast Asia.

Despite being the capital of the state named for the Shan peoples,
the Shan people are a minority in the city, which is comprised largely
of Intha, Pa-O, and Danu ethnic groups. The city also hosts a large
Chinese immigrant population as well as a substantial headquarters of
the Eastern Command of the Tatmadaw (Burmese Army) that occupies

much of the northeast area of the city. By far the largest town in any direction, Taunggyi is a major intersection for trade and, thus, also acts as a cultural, linguistic, religious, and musical crossroads.

Vignette: A Pagoda Festival (Paya pwe).

After spending the night in Taunggyi, I awake at sunrise to the Call to Prayer from one of several mosques serving the small, but audible, local Muslim community. Later that day, a local pagoda festival (*paya pwe*) provides a dynamic display of ethnic expression for some of the local groups. A local wealthy patron has made a sizeable donation to the Shwe Thu Htay Gon Buddhist monastery by procuring a complete copy of the *Tripitaka* (literally the "three baskets"). The *Tripitika* is the body of texts, written in Pali, that record the teachings of Buddhism. The *Tripitika* consists of three parts: the *sutta-pitaka* (discourses of the Buddha and his disciples), the *vinaya-pitaka* (rules and regulations for those who enter the *sangha*), and the *abhidhamma-pitaka* (metaphysical elaborations on the doctrine). These three "baskets" make up the *Tripitika,* or the scriptures of Theravada Buddhism. They are contained in approximately fifty volumes and are said to take approximately two years to recite. Such an important and substantial gift was an opportunity for celebration.

The Buddhist communities surrounding Taunggyi have gathered to commemorate the event with music, dance, and food while the monks recited *sutras* (blessings and prayers) to the donors and for the lay community. While forty or fifty monks began their chanting indoors (heard on CD track 4), a procession of Pa-O musicians, a subgroup of the Karen, (see below) approached the pagoda. Through speakers hung outside of the monastery I could hear the chanting monks outdoors: layers of sound created a festival-like atmosphere. This mobile Pa-O ensemble of seven musicians, each holding a single gong and the last pair holding a large gong slung between them, processed to the pagoda and took position on one side of it (see Figure 3.2). The steady, slow pulsation on the gongs (approximately 12 bpm), set a contemplative tone and were soon joined by a set of cymbals improvising to the measured gong pulses (CD track 17). An elderly male dancer moved to the front of the procession, arms raised high and then alternately thrust in the air at each pulse. The sound was clearly recognizable by all the locals as a Pa-O procession. In addition, the clothing of the Pa-O, dark black or blue baggy trousers and jackets with colorful head scarves was another unmistakable symbol of their group identity.

FIGURE 3.2   *Pa-O Musicians at Shwe Thu Htay Monastery and Pagoda in Taunggyi, Burma/Myanmar. In the background a Shan ozi waits to be played.*

Midway through this performance, not to be outdone, a loud clamor came from the other side of the pagoda, about 70 feet away (CD track 18): faster pulses punched out by many gongs beating approximately 110 bpm. Here a Shan ensemble played for a pair of dancers engaged in a stylized martial arts repartee. The ensemble also consisted of gongs, a pair of cymbals and, the lead instrument, a Shan *ozi*, a long goblet shaped drum as seen in Figure 3.3a and in the background of 3.2. Perhaps ten participants held single gongs each and striking in synchrony while a set of cymbals played a counter rhythm. The *ozi* improvises rhythmic ideas over top. (Douglas fieldnotes)

The Shwe Thu Htay Gon pagoda festival (*paya pwe*) was clearly a special event for the people of the region. The event combined food, dance, family, and friends and reaffirmed relationships between the sangha and the community at large. A wonderful cacophony of sounds—chanting monks, Pa-O processional music and Shan Ozi, amidst the hustle and bustle of old friends reuniting and children playing—performed difference and similarity simultaneously. All were sharing their common Buddhist identity while mildly asserting their unique ethnic identity. One of the most prominent symbols of ethnic identity in the region is the *ozi*.

Ozis can be found throughout much of Burma/Myanmar accompanying folk dances and largely rural festive events. There is great variation in the size, shape, and color of the *ozi* depending on the group playing it; each ethnic minority has adopted certain identifying features. Prominently displayed along one wall of the Shan State Cultural museum in Taunggyi can be found a collection of instruments from several different regional ethnicities (see Figures 3.3 a.b.c.d). The state controlled museum chooses dress and musical instruments as a primary way to mark the ethnic groups in the vicinity: Shan, Palaung, Pao-O, Danu, gongs, and drums are some of the first items one finds upon entering the museum.

ACTIVITY 3.4 *On the CD, I have reproduced recordings I made during my fieldwork. CD tracks 17 and 18 were made at the pagoda pwe discussed above. CD track 19 was recorded the following day with Danu musicians I met at the pwe. The Danu are another ethnic group in the area more closely related to the Burmese than they are to Shan or Pa-O.*

Take listening notes on each of these three tracks, noting as much detail as you can about each—about the number and types of instruments, about the way the instruments relate to each other in terms of timbre, for example. What similarities can you find?

After a close listening to each of them, make a comparative chart so that you can identify how they are similar and different.

In stark contrast to the sounds found at the pagoda festival in northern Burma, a recollection of urban musics further complicates the sounds of Burma/Myanmar's diversity.

Vignette: Karen Carolers. I'm sitting in a small guesthouse in the northern suburbs of Yangon. It's approximately 8 PM on a cool evening of about 65 degrees F, cool enough to cause some of the locals to don long sleeves. The guesthouse is small, with just six rooms catering largely to foreigners. During my visits to Myanmar, it was illegal for foreigners

(a)

(b)

FIGURE 3.3   *A. Shan Ozi; B. Palaung Ozi; C. Pa-O Ozi D. Danu Ozi. The Shan ozi is the longest of all the ozis, stretching 8–10 feet with a head of close to two feet across. The drum is tuned with a tuning paste, weighing down the head to focus the pitch. As it is quite heavy, the ozi is generally played by men and is doubly a marker of masculinity. Although this museum display presents different ozi ensembles, the overwhelming message appears to be one of similarity, rather than one of variance. In this state museum display, participation in the national community is marked; difference is not. Ironically, the music generated from these drums, which is unavailable to the museum patron, does not reveal the same message. The upbeat danceable Shan ozi style contrasts markedly with the serene processional style of the Danu (CD track 19). We will return to some of these ideas of state patronage and presentation in Chapter 4.*

(c)

(d)

FIGURE 3.3   *continued*

to stay anywhere except in government registered guest-houses and hotels. Middle-of-the-night visits to the inn by Military Intelligence verifying this were not uncommon. A bell at the front gate announces some unexpected visitors. A group of 15–20 singers walks up to the front door and sings with strumming guitar accompaniment. Northern Yangon is not far from Insein township where there is a large Karen community. In the International news Karen (pronounced ka-Ren) are best known for their armed resistance to Burmese hegemony that began in 1948 and still lingers today and consequently for their heavy population in refugee camps just over the Thai border. However, they also live in significantly large populations in and around Yangon and south of the city in the Irrawaddy delta. While some are Buddhist, a large percentage of the Karen population is Christian. It was Karen Christians who had come to the guest-house. It was Christmas Eve and they were singing Christmas carols (CD track 20).

Music has always been a central part of Christian worship and has been a primary tool of missionaries to facilitate conversion. This stands in stark contrast to the ambivalent attitude toward singing in Buddhist rituals. Thus, Christian communities, like elsewhere in the world, include a great deal of song as part of their worship. Buddhist monks are forbidden by code in the *vinaya-pitaka* from dancing, music making, and eating after noon and there is very little in the way of Buddhist worship through song on the part of the laity (though there are efforts by some Buddhist musicians to include music as part of Buddhist practice). Most of the Christian churches (Baptist and Catholic) in the country have very little Burman membership but are largely comprised of ethnic Kachin, Chin, and Karen.

Missionaries have had a significant (if contested) presence in the country ever since American Baptists Adoniram and Ann Judson entered Burma in 1813. A legend in Karen animist mythology tells of Y'wa, the divine power and creator, granting books to his children. "Books" in this case is usually understood to mean literacy. The Karen, as the myth is often told, are negligent with the book given to them and it is lost (eaten, stolen, or destroyed, depending on the version). Y'wa offers the Karen the consolation that at some future date their foreign "brothers" will return with the book (or literacy). Many Karen, encouraged by foreign missionaries, saw Baptist missionaries as a fulfillment of this prophecy with the Bible and the literacy developed by the colonial school system as embodying the return of the book. While some Karen retain animistic traditions and some are Buddhism, many today self-identify as Christian. Readers who wish to explore further the relationship between the Karen and Christian missionaries might want to read Amy Tan's novel *Saving Fish From Drowning*.

When the British colonized Burma they extended their control towards the Thai border and many of the Karen subgroups came under their direct control. Christianity and Western-style schools developed and many Karen Christians assumed high positions in the colonial government. In the independence movements of the 20th century, many Karen sided and fought with the British which, after Burmese independence, led to further tensions between the Karen and the Burmese that continue through today. Many English-language histories have cited the introduction of Karen literacy by Protestant missionaries as central to the rise of pan-Karen nationalism. Burmese works, in contrast, tend to present the missionary script as one in a range of different Karen writing systems that appeared in the nineteenth and twentieth centuries. Karen today are spread out over eastern Burma/Myanmar, Yangon and the delta region to the south, in western Thailand (many in refugee camps), and increasingly around the world. Thus, Karen writing serves as a marker of difference and a unifier of Karen-ness not only vis-à-vis the Myanmar and Thai states but also among the disparate Karen groups (see Womack 2005).

While the Karen make up a diverse population within Burma/ Myanmar, their identity today is one very much established in contestation with the Burmese majority. Christianity and Christmas carols become one manifestation of this complicated identity.

MUSIC AND SOCIETY IN THE NORTHEAST, ISAN REGION OF THAILAND

The Lao people are an ethnic subgroup of the Tai. Most of the Lao population lives either in the country of Laos (approximately five million) or in the northeast, Isan, region of Thailand (approximately nineteen million). The Isan region of Thailand comprises seventeen provinces of the northeast along the Mekong River and bordering Laos and Cambodia. Elevated above much of central Thailand, Isan is on the Khorat plateau which rises approximately two hundred meters above sea level and receives significantly less annual rainfall than the lowland areas. Low rainfall to the region's agricultural base makes Isan the poorest area of Thailand.

The main language of the region is Isan, a language quite similar and mutually intelligible with Laotian (in the Tai language family) but written in the Thai alphabet. Though the region's schools and government use the Thai language—often with strong regional accents—the majority of Isan people speak Isan at home. Other dialects and subgroups of Tai and Khmer are also found in the region.

An area such as Isan clearly reveals one of the significant points regarding studying ethnicity; that it is both relational and constantly changing. The historical events that led to the separation of the Lao people across the national borders of Laos and Thailand are various but largely a product of European colonialism. Through treaties with

Siam in 1893 and 1904, France absorbed Laos into French Indochina, which included most of present-day Vietnam and Cambodia. This had significant consequences for many of the Laotian people. The French had not developed Laos economically by the time Laos achieved its own independence in 1954, when Geneva treaties led to the departure of the French from the region. Likewise, the Isan region was a marginalized and neglected part of Thailand. Until a government-backed development drive in the early 1970s brought Bangkok's modernization to what had been the country's most remote and poorest region, life in the northeast was not much different from that in pre-1975 Laos.

The Lao people in both countries share a common language, cuisine, literature, and traditional way of life. Having been separated for most of the last century, however, their lifestyles and cultural identities have strayed apart and are now quite different. The last four decades have seen very different trajectories for the Lao in the two countries. In 1975 the Royal Lao government fell to Communist Pathet Lao, and Laos backslid economically (though is slowly recovering today). In contrast, the Thai government began investing more in the Isan region, successfully incorporating it into the modern Thai state. With the collapse of the Lao economy following the communist coup d'état and the simultaneous modernization of Thailand stemming from its rapid economic growth and internationalization, the cultures of Isan and Laos have diverged significantly over the recent past.

The Isan area of Thailand has long been stereotyped as a place of backward people and poverty. Isan/Lao northeasterners have increasingly migrated to Bangkok to seek work as taxi drivers, gardeners, maids, prostitutes, etc. and other professions which have contributed to the discrimination imposed on many of these migrants by many Bangkok residents of central Thai ethnicity. Despite such longstanding discrimination, more recent years have brought changes in the image of Isan. With increased development, tourist activity, and marketing of its culture the northeast has currently become popular for many Thai and an increasing number of foreigners in search of an "authentic experience." Traditional Lao or Isan music, long denigrated by many central Thai and educated northeasterners, has received favorable attention over the past fifteen years from the national community. Central to this change of image in the national consciousness is Isan's contribution to mainstream Thailand's musical life, especially the country's most exciting popular songs traditions, *luk thung* and *lam sing* (Miller 1998: 316).

ACTIVITY 3.5   *This activity has to do with a video, Two Faces of Thailand (Shanachie) that I hope your school will have available. It is dated but provides an interesting look at relations between the northeast and central Thailand during the 1980s. If you can view the video, take notes related to these questions.*

The narrator occasionally refers to certain behavior as "typically Thai." What does this mean? To what specifically is he referring?

What musical genres are discussed? Briefly describe these genres and discuss how they are used to tease out how music and musical performances is used as a platform to negotiate issues such as rural/urban, traditional/urban, or intergenerational conflict.

What are the two faces of Thailand?

It is said that the two strongest markers of a person's Laotian or Isan identity are that they eat sticky rice (in contrast to much of the dry rice eaten throughout Southeast Asia) and they play the *khaen* (*kaen*), the culture's most important instrument (Figure 3.4, CD track 21). The *khaen* is a free reed aerophone frequently referred to as a mouth organ made from bamboo and wood. It ranges from two to three feet in length. Each of the sixteen bamboo tubes of the standard sized *khaen* has a small reed, and all are enclosed in a hardwood wind chest. The instrument is not unlike the Chinese *sheng* or the Japanese *sho* and sounds similar to a harmonica or an accordion (see Lau 2008 and Wade 2005 in this series). The length and basic pitch of *khaen* construction was not traditionally standardized though that is increasingly done today, especially as the *khaen* is adopted more and more in contemporary musics.

To sound the *khaen*, the instrument is gripped between the heel of each hand, and air is blown into or drawn from (inhaled and exhaled) the wind chest while fingers cover small holes situated just above the wind chest. Covering the holes forces air through the reeds; an uncovered hole will make no sound. As each pipe has a reed (and hole) several finger holes can be covered simultaneously leading to clusters of pitches, drones, and polyphony. This is a characteristic Lao sound (CD track 21).

FIGURE 3.4   *The Khaen played by Khamseung Syhanone*   *(Photograph © Jack Vartoogian/FrontRowPhotos.)*

ACTIVITY 3.6   *The beginning of CD track 21 provides an example of solo* khaen. *Listen for the almost constant sound from the* khaen *created by both inhalation and exhalation. Try and breathe along with Khamseung Syhanone, the* khaen *player. Notice how percussive the breath is.*

   Listen for melody and chord cluster changes in the khaen. *Notice how some notes are held while others provide melodic movement.*

The *khaen* is also found in other four, six, fourteen, and eighteen tubed sizes but sixteen is the most common. The sixteen pipes of the *khaen* play 15 pitches (one doubled at the unison) within a range of two octaves consisting of semitones and whole tones. The physical arrangement of pitches does not appear intuitive to the outsider; it is idiomatic to the playing technique and forms the basis for the theoretical system (see Fig 3.5). The pipe fingerings are organized to avoid a cluster of fingers and to maintain balance on each side, as too many fingers on one side would make the instrument difficult to hold. Different pentatonic scales make up the foundational modes of many Lao songs. Two of the

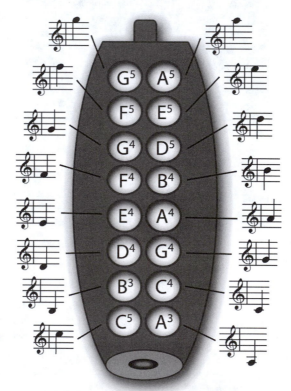

The Khaen and its pitches

FIGURE 3.5 *The Khaen and its pitches*

most common modes (*lai*) are roughly G A C D E (with an emphasis placed on the relationship between C and E) and A C D E G (with an emphasis on the relationship between A and C). Other determining factors of Lao modes include drone notes, chord clusters and final notes. The pipes have been arranged to coordinate with melodic practice, in such a way that three consecutive pipes are avoided in each mode and balance is maintained between the left and the right (Miller 1991: 15–17). As a result of this arrangement, many *khaen* melodies and chords are derived from idiomatic finger placements as much as from a theoretical system. Or, put another way, the theoretical system is built into the fingers of the *khaen*. *Khaen* performance practice and its repertoire has historically been transmitted orally and without a systematic approach though today there are several method books available.

ACTIVITY 3.7 *Following the diagram above, mimic the movements a player would make in order to play a scale.*

$A^3 \ B^3 \ C^4 \ D^4 \ E^4 \ F^4 \ G^4 \ A^4 \ B^4 \ C^5 \ D^5 \ E^5 \ F^5 \ G^5 \ A^5$

Mimic the movements necessary to play each of the two modes. Notice the fairly even distribution on either side of the instrument.

While occasionally played as a solo instrument, the *khaen* is most often used to accompany singing. The most distinctive genres in the Isan area are highly developed forms of poetic repartee call *lam* (CD track 21). Skilled singers, known as *morlam* (*mawlam, molam*), generate a flexible melody coordinated with the lexical tones of the poetry (Lao and Thai being tonal languages). The term *morlam* has come to refer to this style of singing in general.

Lam singers have held a special place in Lao and Isan society. As public singers who memorize and improvise upon vast amounts of poetry, they have played the role of social commentators on diverse aspects of life, including Buddhism, ethical behavior, or local politics.

Lam is a genre of singing that comes in many varieties, depending on region and context. *Lam klawn* (pronounced *lum glahn)* is the most prominent type. It was historically a courting genre in which male-female alternation of playfully poetic lines replete with double entendres, flirtations, and insults would be publicly performed. Participants unprepared with a witty retort or answer could lose face. Many genres of lam today retain the repartee and reenact the courtship, at least as performance. Singers memorize vast amounts of poetry, all written in four-line stanzas with a rhyme scheme peculiar to Lao poetry. An old fashioned performance could start around 9 pm and could continue until sunrise.

> **ACTIVITY 3.8**   *CD track 21* Lam Tan Vey *provides an example of* Lam *from southern Laos. Notice the repartee between the male and female singers, Khamvong Insixiengmai and Thongxhio Manisone.*
>
> *As an exercise in close listening, draw a timeline for the piece that notes the entrance times of the female and male* mawlam. *Sing along with the singer or at least try and identify the pitches they use. Can you put them into either of the two modes mentioned?*

Since the 1980s, traditional *morlam* has had to compete with, but has also fused with several popular genres, the most popular of which is *luk thung*. Often translated as Thai "country music," *luk thung* has played a significant role in reforming the negative stereotypes of the Isan region, as its popularity spans most all of Thailand. The bound-aries—social and sonic—between *luk thung* and *morlam* are quite porous. Many *luk thung* popular singers started their careers singing *lam klawn*.

Singers in Laos and Singers in Thailand.   While the *lam* genres originate with the Lao people, what it means to be ethnically Lao, and what it means to express that ethnicity musically, has changed with the separation of the Lao peoples by the political delineation of Laos and Thailand. Differences in performance styles and context have been created. Singers in Laos, for example, traditionally perform in smaller, more intimate settings than do singers from the Isan area of Thailand. Many Laotian singers and *khaen* players perform seated, often dancing from the waist up, while those in Thailand will stand. Singing and play-ing style in Laos tends to be slower, allowing singers time to think up different melodic patterns.

Though holding a special position in Lao society—primarily because of their knowledge of history, culture, behaviour, Buddhism, etc.—the

Lao *morlam* have traditionally received generally low income from performances and have relatively fewer opportunities for performance (Miller 1998: 343). In recent years, some *morlam* from Thailand have achieved celebrity status as their performances circulate through modern media like CDs, DVDs, and YouTube and MySpace.

ACTIVITY 3.9   *Do an Internet search for video examples of* morlam *and* luk thung. *What similarities can you find with the traditional* lam klawn *on CD track 21?*

HMONG IN VIETNAM, LAOS, AND THAILAND

The Hmong (Mong) ethnic groups provide an interesting comparison and contrast to these upland groups. The communities of Hmong that spread throughout mainland Southeast Asia originally come from Southern China where they are called Miao. From various combinations of political unrest, economic insecurity, and discrimination from the Han Chinese, many left China in the mid 1700s, originally traveling through Vietnam. They can be found throughout Vietnam, Laos, Thailand, and to a lesser degree in Burma/Myanmar. Such migration, over wide space and time, has inevitably led to different cultural patterns and behaviors, yet the Hmong have retained a strong sense of cultural identity primarily through their language and rituals. There are many different subgroups of the Hmong (White Hmong, Flower Hmong, Blue (or Green) Hmong, to name a few) often differentiated by dialect and type of dress.

Until quite recently the Hmong were nonliterate; important cultural knowledge was passed on exclusively in oral form. It was not until the 1950s aided by Western missionaries that the Hmong language, with seven distinct tones, was written down. Several scripts have been used but the Roman alphabet is now the most common.

The Hmong are traditionally slash and burn agriculturalists that shift their cultivation from place to place over the years. For generations they stuck closely to the highland areas and to their tightly knit families and clans (the primary political unit) where they cultivated rice and opium. Regarded as a strong military force, many of them fought for the French during colonization of Vietnam and Laos. Years later during the Vietnam war, despite Laotian neutrality, many Lao Hmong were recruited and trained by CIA forces to fight the growing communist Pathet Lao. After the Pathet Lao victory in 1975, and the reunification of Vietnam under communist rule, many thousands of Hmong fled to refugee camps along the Thai-Lao border. In recognition of their assistance during the Vietnam war, many were able to relocate in Canada, Australia, and France, though by far the largest populations outside of Southeast Asia are found in the United States. This is a direct result of US immigration policy during and after the Vietnam war. Close to 300,000 presently live in the United States, concentrated in California, Minnesota, and Wisconsin.

Music and Language among the Hmong. As language is the primary identity marker that threads through Hmong culture, it is significant that Hmong music is intimately intertwined with Hmong language. It is widely held that words can be "spoken" by musical instruments, and that the poetry for these "words" played instrumentally is identical to that of songs. In other words, Hmong music and Hmong language are inseparable. Hmong people do not distinguish between the sounds we call "music" and the "musical" way that words can be sung. As such, a full understanding of Hmong music—as understood by the Hmong—would necessitate a command of the language. With seven tones in the language, there is a natural melodic contour to regular Hmong speech in all of its dialects.

The Qeej. The *qeej* (pronounced "gaeng") is the most important musical instrument in Hmong culture. Like the Laotian *khaen* it is a free reed aerophone made from long bamboo pipes (Figure 3.6, CD track 22). While in appearance and pronunciation (though not the spelling of its name) the *qeej* may appear to be quite similar to the other free reed aerophones of Southeast Asian ethnic groups, to the Hmong, the function, sound, and importance of the *qeej* is unique to their culture. Any similarity of form between the *qeej* and the *khaen* is misleading. The uniqueness of the *qeej* is found in its ability to express the innate lyrical qualities of the tonal Hmong language in which pitch contour of syllables is pertinent to the lexical meaning. For the Hmong, the key distinction between their instrument and those of other ethnic groups lies in the ability of a *qeej* player to literally "speak" through the instrument. The *qeej* is not a musical instrument per se but rather a voice.

To know the true history and culture of the Hmong, you should take it from the *qeej*, claim the Hmong. While the *qeej* is similar in

FIGURE 3.6   *Song Vue Chang plays Hmong qeej, Providence RI 1981. The qeej has six tone-producing pipes, a wooden wind chest, and a seventh long pipe that serves as the mouthpiece. Each of the six pipes contains a free reed, which, like the khaen reeds, vibrates when a finger-hole is covered. The qeej produces a continuous sound when the player both inhales and exhales.   (Photo © Amy Catlin.)*

construction to other Southeast Asian free reed bamboo instruments, only the Hmong use it to communicate to the spirit world. Hmong cultural identity is closely linked to the retention of their language and the *qeej* that speaks the language to the ancestor is, not surprisingly, an important cultural symbol for Hmong in Southeast Asia and abroad. Not only does it signify Hmong-ness among the living community and connect diasporic Hmong to their homeland, but also its ability to speak to spirits connects the present ethnic identity to one deeply rooted in oral tradition.

ACTIVITY 3.10   *Re-read this section on the Hmong and the* qeej. *Every time you see the word "*qeej*" speak it out loud saying "gaeng."*

The Hmong language has seven tones: contours and relative pitches of vowels that will establish differences in meaning. Each of these seven tones can be replicated on the Hmong *qeej* along with all of the Hmong vowel sounds (not the consonants). Used in various combinations the pipes create a single tone-word and eventually can communicate (in a literal not symbolic sense) entire sentences and ideas. Though the *qeej* "speaks" in Hmong, not all Hmong will know how to interpret the sounds into understandable words. Master *qeej* players know how to make the *qeej* speak and they are also the ones with the most understanding and skill when it comes to the communication of the *qeej*.

This form of speaking with the *qeej* demands that finger positions for different pitches are to be memorized for each word in the Hmong language. Players memorize the language as it is spoken on the *qeej*. This is not considered music in the aesthetic "enjoyable sense,"—not unlike other religious chant I have discussed above—nor is it considered an act of creation or improvisation, as specific texts are being uttered.

ACTIVITY 3.11   *Listen to the qeej recording of a new year's song, "Qeej Kawm Ntawv" found on CD track 22. This excerpt is played by Boua Xou Mua a spiritual leader and former chief of a Blue Hmong village. Compare the recording of the* qeej *to that of the Laotian* khaen. *What similarities of sound can you identify?*

What are the most significant sonic distinctions?

Though recent changes of the Hmong living conditions have changed musical practice (see forthcoming chapters) the traditional function of the *qeej* is still largely for formal events. Performed primarily at cultural events like new year, weddings, and, most importantly, funerals, the *qeej*'s role is to communicate with the spirits. Using the *qeej* for other purposes including entertainment has—traditionally—held no value in Hmong culture.

During a Hmong funeral, the most important context for performance, the *qeej* is played continuously for many days. The soul of the deceased must join with the ancestors and the *qeej* is essential to facilitating that end. The animist world-view of the Hmong involves a complex cosmology that includes "multiple personal souls, ancestral spirits, spirit helpers, spirit demons, and distant gods of good and evil" (Morrison 1998). Maintaining personal and community health involves proper attendance to these invisible forces that can have significant influence on the mundane world.

The role of the *qeej* during a funeral is to pacify the dead spirit by guiding the departed soul to the home of the ancestral spirits. This simultaneously offers comfort to those left behind. The musician's dress includes an elaborate metal necklace, which tinkles as he performs the mandatory dance movements while playing. In the funerary ritual the dance is called *dhiam qeej tawj qeej* (jumping *qeej*, spinning *qeej*). In this, the *qeej* player dances while playing, with each gesture having a meaning. The dance evokes a metaphorical journey to the ancestors from the material world. These movements include spinning, to confuse evil spirits that may try to prevent the soul of the deceased from joining his ancestors, and larger circular patterns, which indicate the journey on horseback of the soul (see Catherine Falk 2003). When the soul departs for the ancestors' world, the *qeej* carefully guides it away, so that it cannot present a threat to the clan (Thao 2006, 256 also Morrison 1998).

In recent years, and in diaspora contexts, the dance has worked itself into secular contexts. Especially during New Year, competitions are routinely held for the best dancers. Such secular, enjoyable contexts challenge the traditional role and symbolism of *qeej* playing and add new meanings to the tradition.

ACTIVITY 3.12 *Find a performance of* qeej *playing and dancing from an online video source (YouTube, Google Video). Or watch Amy Catlin's film* Hmong Musicians in America: Interactions with Three Generations of Hmong Americans 1978–1996 *(see the resources at the end of this book). Watch the dance and reflect on the meanings that the dance and the sounds have.*

If you live in California, Montana, Minnesota, or Washington State, folk festivals often feature qeej *performances. Keep an eye out.*

As the Hmong language has only recently been set to script, and oral tradition has been the primary source of authority, there is much confusion regarding historical accuracy. Hmong scholar Gayle Morrison below reflects on her own teacher's warnings of the problems in deciphering true history. Morrison writes:

> With great candor and concern for the accurate documentation of Hmong culture, Mr. Kue encouraged me to be cautious in my research, and to verify that a source person actually knows what he or she is talking about. He emphasized that, since the Hmong did not have a written language previously, it is difficult to prove anything. Mr. Kue told me that he himself has no proof of what he has told me, but he believes his stories are true because he translates them directly from the qeej. From generation to generation, changes take place in all other aspects of Hmong culture, but not in the ancient and unaltered language of the qeej. As Mr. Kue noted, "If you want to know the true history and culture of the Hmong, then you should take it from the qeej."
>
> (Morrison 1998)

The language of the *qeej* songs holds their entire cultural body of cosmological knowledge. Not surprisingly, expert *qeej* players are highly respected for their skills and the crucial knowledge that they hold.

ACTIVITY 3.13 *What other examples can you think from your own life regarding the role of instruments in asserting or retaining a distinct cultural ethnic identity? What roles do guitars, accordians, etc. play in the performance of ethnicity? Can you point to how these symbols change from generation to generations or from region to region.*

CONCLUSION

In this chapter I have presented just a tiny glimpse into the ethnic complexity of mainland Southeast Asia and hinted at how this diversity relates to our other themes of globalization and political struggle. Each identity is fostered relationally vis-a-vis the state and other neighboring groups. The historical development of ethnic identity in many cases (Karen, Hmong, etc.) is also intimately tied to the relationship between colonial and neo-colonial powers (British, French, American) and the dominant ethnic group. Difference is often asserted with marked symbols (distinct instruments or dress) or adoption of something regional with a slight local spin (such as different *ozis* and free reed aerophones) leading to heightened ethnic expression through music. Many of these groups suffer economic and political hardship and may not have abundant resources to devote to music, however, music still plays an important role in preserving cultural identity. Others find identification (and cultural capital) through global trends (as in Christian music or connecting with a national popular music). In each case presented above music is embedded deeply into different ways of living as people make music useful and meaningful in their lives. Music here cannot be separated from courtship, worship, rituals, festivals or ethnic politics.

As political and economic opportunities change, so too does the music. The very existence of this music on commercial CDs, on YouTube, and in this textbook, speaks to changing circulation of the music and to changing meanings. In Chapters 4 and 5 I now move more explicitly to the politicization and globalization of many of these local traditions.

CHAPTER 4

Music and Political Turmoil

Activities in Chapter 1 revealed that many Western perspectives of Southeast Asia highlight a plethora of negative images: oppression, dictatorships, poverty, war, and prostitution among others. It should be obvious by now that there is much, much more to this area. Without a doubt, however, there has been significant political turmoil in the region over the past fifty years. Musicians, audiences, and their musical behavior have contributed to both political aggression and to political conciliation in countless ways, and mainland Southeast Asia is a rich area for exploring the relationships between political activity and music.

Numerous questions arise in regard to Southeast Asian political turmoil. What are the roots of these hardships? Can we generalize across the region? How, and in what different ways, has music played a role in political struggle? Has music inspired people to fight for change or has it comforted people with the status quo? Has it helped them recover from various atrocities, healed rifts, built bridges or reinforced social boundaries? What have the consequences of political upheaval been on music making in these communities? What roles have governments taken towards musicians and music culture at large? This chapter will explore music and politics from two occasionally clashing perspectives: that of the state in relation to its people and to the rest of the world, and secondly that of the people in contrast to the state.

Certainly the countries of Burma/Myanmar, Thailand, Cambodia, and Vietnam have had more than their share of struggle over the past century. Unlike other war-torn parts of the world, the roots of many of these conflicts cannot be found in lack of resources or food. These countries are not short on natural resources and, given the consistent monsoon rains, are not typically prone to drought or famine. Poverty and conflict have, rather, been a result of wars between neighboring countries, internal struggles over access, foreign wars played out on their soil, ideological struggles, uneven distribution of resources, and poor economic management. Charismatic personalities of particular leaders and despots have motivated and catalyzed many of the most important political and ideological movements.

> ACTIVITY 4.1   *Search online for histories and biographies to learn who are the most influential people in each country of main-land Southeast Asia. Find three people of significance to share with your classmates: one politician, one artist, and one musician. Explain how each has been influential, whether for good, for bad, or both.*
>
> *Some histories might include these names but you might find others: Ne Win, Aung San Suu Kyi, Aung San, Chulalongkor, Mongkut, Bhumibol Adulyadej, Pol Pot, Hun Sen, Hồ Chí Minh, Luang Wichitwathakan, or Plaek Pibulsonggram.*

FROM THE TOP DOWN: COLONIALISM, INDEPENDENCE, AND NATION BUILDING

While I do not wish to dwell too long on the fascinating history of Southeast Asia, it is important to understand that many of the ongoing struggles found in the area are rooted in the transition from colonial holdings to modern nation-states. The process of shedding the colonial (British and French) yokes, of adopting contemporary governments in place of feudal kingships and of negotiating power relations among diverse ethnic groups help explain many of the complicated political situations that exist today. The departures of British colonial powers from Burma and of French powers from Laos, Cambodia, and Vietnam were difficult, protracted affairs. While often violent, they did produce and encourage the assertion of a national identity distinct from those of the colonial powers and neighboring countries. A pertinent component of that nation building is the musical production that accompanied it.

Anthems.   One insight into the independence struggles and state for-mation can be found in national anthems. While these countries contain unique groups of people with a dazzling variety of music, the process of nationalizing (uniting a community around shared symbols) here takes on a character that is similar to other nations throughout the world. Think of the symbols a nation-state would use as emblems for its people (flags, anthems, currency, statues, etc.). An examination of national anthems reveals not only the ways in which a country joins the global community, that is by adopting a global type of symbol, but also, often, ways in which a degree of uniqueness and difference is asserted.

Burma, for example, declaring independence from Britain in 1948, chose for its national anthem the most popular song of the independence movement. The *Dobama (Our Burma)* song was a call for uniting Burmese identity against the British and was the unofficial pre-independence anthem between 1941 and 1945. Song recitals—at which the audience was taught the melody and meaning of the song—were rallying points for anti-colonial propaganda (Khin Yi 1988). In 1948 the song "Kaba Ma Kyei" ("Till the End of the World") was adopted as the national anthem. It was written by a member of the Young Man's Buddhist Association, YMBA Sayar Tin. "Kaba Ma Kyei" is written in a style popular in its day that mixes Burmese playing styles with Western instrumentation and harmony—today this style is referred to as *kit haung* (oldie) music. After so many decades of colonialism it made sense that the song had a very international sound and was easily performed with piano or marching band arrangement.

In 1932 Phra Chen Duriyanga, one of the first cultural ministers of democratic Thailand, composed the music of the Thai national anthem in a similarly international style. Duriyanga was trained in Western music and enjoyed the Western-style jazz-influenced popular music that was circulating throughout the urban centers in the first half of the 20th century.

The anthem of Cambodia, "Nokoreach," derives its name from an ancient Khmer kingdom and was adapted (in 1941 and restored after 1993) and modernized from an old folk tune into something that is recognizably international, i.e., polyphonic and adapted for marching bands and chorus. Here the Khmer anthem embodies one of the profound temporal contradictions of modern nationalism: simultaneously deeply ancient and very modern.

During the 1940s there were a large number of patriotic songs composed in Vietnam, many of which were modeled after marches and French military band music. These marches and songs made a strong impression on young Vietnamese yearning for their country's independence (Gibbs 2000). One of them, "Tien Quan Xa" (Onward Soldiers) composed by Văn Cao, became the North Vietnamese anthem in 1944. After unification in 1976, Hồ Chí Minh selected "Tien Quan Ca" as the anthem for the entire nation.

All of the anthems, sung in the language of the dominant ethnic group, aim to symbolically unify these countries, yet they are based on styles and traditions from well beyond their borders. What does that say about nationalism at large?

ACTIVITY 4.2   *Listen online to the national anthems of each country in mainland Southeast Asia.*

See <national-anthems.net>

Compare and contrast them to other national anthems with which you are familiar in terms of musical style, rendition, and lyrics if available.

What sonic relations do these pieces have with other Southeast Asian music you have already studied? Are there any similarities to the musics from the royal court heard on CD tracks 6, 9, 11, 12?

A major challenge for these countries during the past century was the creation of a "modern" image of the country that had unquestionable ties to important historical icons such as kings and empires. National identity was created partly through the appropriation of Western ideology and techniques but also by simultaneously opposing Western domination (see Tarling 2001:5). This process of nationalizing was also felt through a process of classicization of many music traditions.

Classicization: The Creation of Nation Through Art Music.   As these states moved from colonial or feudal entities to contemporary nation-states, a process of musical nationalization included unifying some commonly (though not universally) held musics and musical values. While the specific stories of decolonization and modernizing differ from country to country, the government of each "new" country made concerted efforts to patronize certain styles and traditions of music. Nationalization is necessarily relational in that the manner in which a nation asserts its difference is similar to the manner by which another nation does the same. Several trends that could be found across the region, as implied above, the concept of the flag or the anthem—and even the basic structure of each—isn't questioned, as each country adopts its own version of the concept.

Nationalization, as distinct from fostering allegiance to a feudal kingship, has often involved the middle class populous (or a comparatively affluent citizenry) in reinforcing state symbols. While the term "classical" is problematic in reference to the historically rooted musical traditions of the area, "classicization"—the process of making traditions palatable for middle class taste—is a useful way of discussing changes in musical patronage. A classicized tradition, according to scholar Partha Chatterjee, is one that has been "reformed, reconstructed, fortified against charges of barbarism and irrationality" through the process of selection and elevation of particular cultural symbols and behaviors (Chatterjee 1993:127). For other scholars, this kind of classicization is a form of sanitizing and systematizing, tied to the negotiation of history and a sense of the past and a covert means of controlling populations. Such projects make the world not only more "legible," but also more controllable (see Scott 1998). These perspectives point to two important themes of classicization—the presentation to other nations of refined and reformed culture, and the sanitizing, organizing and standardizing of internal diversity. These processes provide the content for a nationalized cultural identity driven largely by middle class tastes (see also Moro 2004).

The state-inspired projects directed at musical classicization included many endeavors such as: new forms of musical transmission, mass education systems, standardization efforts, writing and notation systems, institutionalization of music theory and scholarship, public concerts and competitions, and adoption of print and electronic media. All of these new projects are to be found throughout the global community of nations and are most often tied to the middle class and nationalist movements.

In mainland Southeast Asia the past century has seen a wealth of state-controlled projects designed to organize musical life, behavior, transmission, creation, and aesthetics. These include new training academies, standardized repertoire, canonized curricula, written musical notation, the development of a specialized and standardized musical vocabulary (often Sanskrit-language based), national composing and performing competitions, and a host of other frameworks. It is certainly the case that the ideas and institutions that lead to and govern such classicizing were (and are) part of the global flow of financial and economic markets and their accompanying ideologies of progress and growth. This process has resulted in the ironic mix of Western-derived elements with selected elements of ancient or pre-colonial history—globally-informed aesthetics with locally determined manifestations.

The effort to assert a distinct political unit (the nation) has largely been accomplished through globally defined parameters regarding what the nation should be. Many of the global influences on music in mainland Southeast Asian will be discussed in Chapter 5. Here I will focus on some specific gestures these Southeast Asian nation-states have made in an effort to create national symbols out of their music.

Thailand, or Siam at the time, was not formally colonized by European powers. Yet the influence of the French and British colonial powers on Siam's doorstep throughout the 19th and early 20th century was paramount. In response, Siam, led by King Chulalongkorn discussed further below, made great efforts in the early part of the century to construct a national identity based on a centralized culture—a centralized culture that needed, in some measure, to be created. In contrast to the strategies of many other countries, traditional Thai court music was not embraced as an emblem in the 1930s and 40s by the new democracy; it was considered by certain policy makers as primitive or unrefined. Instead, Western style forms and genres rooted in military march music, ballroom dancing, jazz, etc., were more prevalent. The present Thai king himself, coming of age in the 1940s, formed a palace jazz band to learn clarinet and alto saxophone. He composed and performed many pieces in this style and has traveled widely with his music, playing jazz with Benny Goodman, Jack Teagarden, Lionel Hampton, and others.

ACTIVITY 4.3   *Search online video/audio websites for recordings of the king of Thailand (Bhumibol Adulyadej or Rama IX) playing American-style jazz.*

If you looked at the history of Rama IX in activity 4.1 review your material. If you didn't, do a brief bit of research to learn who Bhumibol Adulyadej is.

Only in recent years (since the 1970s) has government patronage of music in Thailand shifted its attention to the traditional court music with the creation of music departments in many universities that embrace Thai classical styles. This can be largely credited to the process of classicization and the growing middle class in the country that has increasingly forged global relations while, at the same time, sought to assert a unique musical history rooted in local histories. Contemporary movies such as *The Overture* (see Activity 4.4) have also contributed to a revival of *piphat* ensembles.

Defense against many foreign musics has been one of the primary reasons for Burma/Myanmar and Cambodia to patronize the arts during the past two decades. Governments of both countries fear a moral degradation brought on by international pop culture. For example, the first of several goals of the Ministry of Culture and Fine Arts, a state-run cultural institution of the Royal Government of Cambodia, aims "to block the anarchic influx of foreign cultures into Cambodia by passing and regulating laws to control the imports and exposures of foreign cultures to the Khmer public" (Norodom 2000, see also Sam 2003). These laws aim to create "morality and kindness within the people by means of performing arts, which are effective educational tools." Similarly, the State Peace and Development Council (SPDC) of Myanmar generated numerous projects in the mid 1990s (new arts university, national competitions, notation projects, see Figure 4.1) associated with two national objectives—"uplift of the morale and morality of the entire nation" and "uplift of national prestige and integrity and preservation and safeguarding of cultural heritage and national character" (see Douglas 2003a, 2003b). An example of this discourse can be found in the closing address of the annual performing arts competitions where Secretary 1- Lt General Thein Sein asserts that the "preservation of fine traditions is an auspicious act leading to further glorifying national pride.

THE NEW LIGHT OF MYANMAR Saturday, 3 October, 1998   7

Patron of the Leading Committee for Organizing the Sixth Myanma Traditional Performing Arts Competitions Secretary-1 Lt-Gen Khin Nyunt attends harp contest. — MNA

FIGURE 4.1 *Press clipping of a senior military officials attending the National Performing Arts Competition in Burma/Myanmar.*

As glorification of national pride in turn further vitalizes nationalist fervour (sic), it is strength reinforcing the national might that is always ready to safeguard the interest of our nation and people at any time." (*New Light of Myanmar*, Nov 5 2004).

The above material provides a number of ways by which governments, through policies and patronage, play a role in shaping a musical culture. I will move shortly to some examples of local, grassroots musical behavior that defies the agenda of the state. First, however, I'd like to reflect on some of the personal negotiations necessary for musicians involved in state projects. How do musicians, political agents themselves, negotiate such top-down control from the state?

Mainland Southeast Asia provides a confusing variety of state sponsored projects designed to support particular traditions, fend off globalization, maintain the precedence of a particular ethnic group or class, and/or create jobs for musicians. The social contexts of the performing and composing musician among different state projects is diverse. The variety of reactions to these projects range from excitement to disgust. While most musicians (of classical or court musics) yearn for government patronage, the political costs of accepting such patronage are not always desired.

Discussing the plethora of new state-sponsored music projects in Burma one eighty-year old musician said to me, "I wish I were twenty years old. It's a great time to be a musician. There are more jobs available now then ever before." In contrast, a slightly younger professional musician aggressively reacted, "I want nothing to do with these corrupt government projects. They don't care about the music. It's just for the generals to show off. Graduates from the new university will never have careers in music and winners of the national competition are not the best players." As he suggested, patronage of music through official government sources is never evenly distributed across the variety of musicians, traditions, or locales and is often used for non-musical ends. My experience is paralleled by Miranda Arana's who, in her quest to study Vietnamese music was told by a senior musicologist to "avoid musicians trained at the National Music Conservatory" (Arana 1999:4).

One progressive and important change brought on by many state projects, particularly in the competition and educational contexts, is the role of women in the court traditions. While historically cultivated as a hobby the opportunities for pursuing professional careers in music has increased significantly for women. This change has been most prominent in the male dominated theatrical and ritual musics and the ensembles (such as *saing waing*) that have led them. While I did not find all female *saing waing* troupes in the rural areas there are an increasing number of women performers found in the annual Sokayeti performing arts competition and at the state university.

For some, government-inspired projects are reductions or simplifications designed to create useful symbols for use in other political contexts. State-imposed simplifications and standardizations (taxation, transportation, education, law, etc.), as James Scott asserts, are the basic givens of modern statecraft (Scott 1998). They make the world not only more "legible," but also more controllable. State simplifications, however, acting somewhat like abridged maps, do not successfully represent the actual activity of the society; they represent only that slice of it that interests the official observers. These maps, Scott continues, are "maps that, when allied with state power...enable much of the reality they depict to be remade" (Scott 1998:3). Music competitions, schools and universities, and standardized notations, as state *selections* of tradition, are chosen to present, or to map, "tradition" for the nation and international community. They also serve to make musical culture more controllable.

In 2004, a highly acclaimed film called *Homrong* (*The Overture*) was released in Thailand. The film is loosely based upon the biography of *ranāt* (xylophone) player Luang Pradit Phairao (1881–1954). While much of the film deals with his rising success, teaching moral lessons of confidence and arrogance along the way, the later half of the film dramatizes the struggles of an artist who resists state arts policies. After the 1932 coup Field Marshal Plaek Pibulsonggram (known as Por) banned classical Thai music and other forms of traditional culture. As Prime Minister and military dictator of Thailand from 1938 to 1944, Marshal Plaek enforced modernist policies encouraging Western attire, Western education, and a variety of non-Thai cultural practices. Such policies were necessary, according to Marshal Plaek, to convince foreigners that Thailand was not an undeveloped and barbaric country. Thailand, in his mind, needed to be recognized by foreigners as a civilized and modernized country. Artists such as Luang Pradit Phairao had to negotiate such policies with their own sense of modernization, tradition, and Thai-ness.

This period of Thai history poses a fundamental question of national politics in the face of globalization. To what degree must a country abandon its long-held traditions in order to be respected and regarded as an equal in the national community? Thai court music, with its monarchial associations, was one of many arenas where such arguments about national culture were played out. Marshal Plaek restricted many traditions in an effort to move the country "forward," while Sorn, the lead character of *The Overture* asserts in response that "a large tree can stand against a storm, only with deep and strong roots."

ACTIVITY 4.4 *If you are able to obtain a copy, watch the Thai film* The Overture *based on the life of Luang Pradit Phairao. Reflect on the significance that such a historical drama might have on Thai music today. Compare and contrast the depictions of "modernization" in* The Overture *and* The King and I *(see Activity 5.3).*

COUNTER STATE MUSICS: FROM THE PEOPLE UP

In contrast to the government controlled, top-down strategies of unification, simplification, or national cultural defense, there are countless examples of individuals (or groups) who challenge government policies through music. Here I shall highlight some examples of musicians resisting government controls, starting with Burma/Myanmar.

In Burma/Myanmar today, the military regime maintains a draconian hold on all types of expression. All materials to be published (books, magazines, films, CDs, etc.) are scrutinized by a press censor board. In the 1960s when dictator General Ne Win banned all Western music as "decadent," a popular underground culture known as "stereo" music sprang up to compete with the "mono" music played on state radio. As this grassroots popular tradition began to grow, several notable artists established strong followings. Sai Htee Saing, backed by his band, Thabawa Yinthwenge (The Wild Ones), became one of the most popular singers of the late 1970s and 1980s. Sai Htee Saing was ethnic Shan from Shan state and sang songs in both Shan and Burmese with a distinct accent. His soft rock songs often led with acoustic guitar became very popular among the lowland Burmese, introducing many Burmese to elements of Shan life. Many of his lyrics were thought to contain discreet social messages through hidden meanings. During the 1980s, Sai Htee Saing was considered not only a master songwriter but very skilled in eluding the infamous censor board. Many of his songs focused on the civil war and the struggle of life in his homeland.

In the 1990s he succumbed to government pressure to promote state ideology through his songs and performances. Like other musicians who curried favor with the generals he soon gained special privileges, and was seen regularly in the state press with junta leaders (whose legitimacy was reinforced through his popularity). By singing songs often written by military officials that endorsed government ideology Sai Htee Saing lost much of his audience. While his albums from the 1980s still sell remarkably well today, his credibility has diminished significantly. Despite the lingering popularity of many of his songs, his contradictory career is a clear example of the contrast between state resistance and state endorsement; between popular hero and sell out. He died in 2008, but his songs continue to be heard and, thanks to the Internet, are now distributed wider than ever.

The Myanmar censor board throughout the 1980s directed most of its attention towards lyrics and visual presentation, and took a fairly ambivalent role towards contemporary musical styles. Musicians were not restricted from playing electric guitars and synthesizers, but the government did monitor how they were played. Artists with long hair and provocative dress were consistently restricted from print and television media. However, despite the government efforts to contain these "decadent" images, they still circulated among the Burmese youth hungry for foreign musics.

Though considered "decadent," global styles of folk, rock and roll, and especially heavy metal in the 80s and 90s and rap today, are readily available through pirate cassette circulation, and have provided fodder for 100s of copy songs. "Copy songs," as they are called in Burma/Myanmar, are essentially cover versions of contemporary hits from the U.S., Europe, and Japan. Burmese versions of songs are easily found across the pop spectrum; from Madonna, to Bruce Springsteen, Jay-Z to Avril Lavigne, Celine Dion to Ludacris. However, lyrics for these remade copy songs usually have nothing to do with the original song meaning and are typically benign love songs completely absent of social commentary (despite an aggressive heavy metal or hip hop sound).

Inside the country it is, thus, difficult to find mass mediated music that speaks out against the oppressive junta. A Bob Dylan- or Bruce Springsteen-like social commentator would be thrown in jail in the Burmese context. Following the 1988 events, censorship laws intensified for popular musicians. By June 1991 an additional censorship board had been set up under the Ministry of Home and Religious Affairs to scrutinize not only the lyrics, but also the rendition and the musical arrangement of songs to protect Burmese traditions from foreign influences "undermining national spirit and patriotism and making Myanmar culture extinct" (Smith 1991, 54). Musicians, filmmakers, and artists of all varieties were commanded by senior generals to work, as their patriotic duty, with the state-controlled Myanmar Music Organization. Since "music is an effective public relations instrument," the generals claimed that "the public could be organized with the strength of music" (quoted from Smith 1991, 54).

I remember a visit to the Myanmar censor board in 2005. Aung Wei needed to pick up the results of his application in person. Aung Wei was the drummer of a moderately successful Yangon rock band. He and his band were finishing up a recording and needed to get clearance from the censor board before it could be released. A complete version of the piece to be published (whether it be CD, magazine, video or book) needs to be vetted before it can be mass-produced. If the board does not approve of the contents then an entire project can be spoiled with all the money invested into that project lost. Such a moment is always tense for Burmese musicians as there is little indication from month to month on how aggressively the committee will critique their submission. Not knowing exactly what is acceptable from day to day, and trying to anticipate how the board might interpret poetic lyrics forces many writers to be quite conservative for fear of losing the entire project. The burden of censorship thus falls to a significant degree, then, upon the artists/writers themselves. Such self-censorship (based on fear of the consequences) is more effective at controlling dissent than the activities of the censor board themselves.

After a long wait in the car with other musicians sympathetic to his nervousness, Aung Wei finally returned. All of his songs were cleared except for one song with the term "night club" in it. He wasn't sure exactly why it was not allowed. Did it point to foreign influence? decadent lifestyle? partying? Did it clash with traditional values (as determined by the state), as it surely didn't clash with youth behavior? Aung Wei was not given an explanation and, having been through the process before, he didn't care. It was a minor enough infraction to fix (either with a silent patch or a voice over) and it would not tank his project. Others are not so lucky.

ACTIVITY 4.5   *Freemuse is an independent international organization that advocates freedom of expression for musicians* *and composers worldwide. Visit their website www.freemuse. com and use the search function to not only search via country but by the traditions or artists that I have introduced you to. Read the collection of (usually very short) articles for each of the countries under discussion here. Form a discussion group with a few of your classmates and, based on material there for mainland Southeast Asian countries, formulate answers to the following questions.*

What examples can you find of censoring popular musicians, traditional musicians, ethnic minorities or foreign artists/ styles?

For what types of reasons does censorship happen? What concerns are generalizable across the area and which ones are specific to particular nations?

When does it appear to be justifiable to censor material?

Many musicians have found that in order to express themselves freely they must leave the country. Mun Awng, for example, left the country after participating in the 1988 protests. He now lives in Norway and, like many exiled Burmese, is unable to make his living as a musician. Nonetheless, he is actively engaged in the prodemocracy movement abroad and sings regularly for benefits and awareness-raising events. In 2004 a benefit CD was put together by the activist organization U.S. Campaign for Burma. The album, *For the Lady,* is dedicated to "freeing Aung San Suu Kyi and the courageous people of Burma" (Figure 4.2) and contains mostly previously-released tracks by Paul McCartney, REM, Avril Lavigne, Ani DiFranco, Eric Clapton, Sting, U2, and many others. Mun Awng is the only Burmese artist to appear on the recording; he sings the song "Tempest of Blood" on the last track on the double album. "Tempest of Blood" was written by Min Ko Naing, one of the student leaders of the 1988 uprising who has since spent over 15 years in prison as a result of leading demonstrations against the military leaders. The opening line of the song, "the blood that was shed on the streets will never disappear" speaks directly to shared Burmese experiences— experience that could never be published or sung about in the country today.

FOR THE LADY

Dedicated to freeing Aung San Suu Kyi
and the courageous people of Burma

PAUL McCARTNEY • PEARL JAM • STING

ANI DIFRANCO • R.E.M. • BONNIE RAITT

U2 • ERIC CLAPTON • PETER GABRIEL

COLDPLAY • AVRIL LAVIGNE • MANÁ

MATCHBOX TWENTY • DAMIEN RICE

INDIGO GIRLS • MUN AWNG • TRAVIS

BETTER THAN EZRA • TALIB KWELI

LILI HAYDN • THE NIGHTWATCHMAN

GUSTER • BEN HARPER • HOUR CAST

REBECCA FANYA • BRIGHT EYES

NATALIE MERCHANT

FIGURE 4.2   *For the Lady. CD produced by US Campaign for Burma.*

ACTIVITY 4.6   *Look online for a copy of the playlist on the* For the Lady *CD and for a copy of the song "Tempest of Blood". Share your knowledge of these contemporary Western popular songs with your classmates. Many of the songs have nothing to do with Burma/Myanmar while others make veiled references to the situation in the country. What commentary do these artists and their songs make on the situation in Burma? In what ways are albums such as this a benefit to the furthering of the cause for Burmese people? Do they offer a service to the cause? This double album only contains one track by a Burmese musician—is that a problem? Be prepared to debate this with classmates who might not agree.*

The U2 song "Walk On," the first song on the album, is banned in Burma. Find a copy of the lyrics online. If you were a member of the Myanmar press scrutiny board charged with controlling public dissent would you censor this song? Why or why not?

Vietnam. For many Americans "Vietnam" is a war and the "Music of Vietnam" is American rock protest music. The war played a significant role in American popular culture and was critiqued and explored from countless vantage points in American songs throughout the late 1960s and 1970s. American rock was "not only the soundtrack of opposition to the war; it was the soundtrack of the war itself" (Garafalo 2007; 3). Ironic, though not surprising, is the fact that most Vietnamese refer to the same war as the "American War." American music from this period thus holds a paradoxical place in Vietnamese society, being simultaneously the music of a foreign invading power and a music with strong anti-war associations. From the Vietnamese perspective, the "American War" had significant musical impact on music making and music composition in Southeast Asia. The huge influx of American music—found wherever American soldiers congregated—was consumed and imitated by numerous Vietnamese artists before, and even after, the fall of Saigon in 1975.

Three of the most significant composers/songwriters during the war era (1960–75) were Phạm Duy, Văn Cao, and Trịnh Công Sơn. Though there were of course many others, these three provide interesting contrasts.

Phạm Duy is least remembered in Vietnam today as he fled the country and emigrated to the United States shortly after the end of the American War. He composed prolifically during his period in exile. While his pieces were banned back in Vietnam he is perhaps the best-known composer among the Vietnamese diaspora (see Wong 2004). Phạm returned to Vietnam in 2005 at the age of 85 and continues to compose.

"In Vietnam, everything—music, poetry—has to do with politics. You cannot avoid it. If you didn't have this situation in Vietnam, you wouldn't have *me*," said Phạm Duy in an interview with Deborah Wong (Wong 2003: 135). Phạm Duy's entire musical career reflects the tumultuous 20th century history of Vietnam. It began with his singing and playing guitar with a *cải lương* theater troupe. *Cải lương* is a style of theater that combines traditional theater with the increasingly popular French and European musics of the 1910s and 20s (CD track 16). In the late 1910s and 1920s these performances would often include two ensembles, one of traditional instruments and one of Western instruments (I will return to *cải lương* in Chapter 5). Phạm Duy spent several years studying music in Paris in the 1950s and then returned to Vietnam to compose pieces that mixed a variety of traditional, popular and Western styles. While formally trained in the Western compositional style he also devoted significant attention to collecting and documenting traditional Vietnamese music. In 1975 he published one of the first English language books on the subject titled *Musics of Vietnam*.

Phạm Duy has consistently resisted being pigeon-holed into a specific political stance, indeed it was his refusal to ascribe to specific ideologies that forced his departure from Vietnam and also created difficulties for him in his life in the US. For years the Vietnamese government banned his compositions, yet his refusal to associate himself with the far-right ideology of the U.S. based Vietnamese expatriate community and his decisions to return to Vietnam repeatedly gave rise to accusations that he was pro-communist—despite his consistent condemnation of extremist perspectives.

In many of his compositional works Phạm Duy sought to transcend political factionalism. A nationalist at heart, his "National Road" (Con Đường Cái Quan) song cycle, started in 1954 and completed in 1960, for example, is a set of 19 songs (in three sections) that symbolically wind their way from the Chinese border in Northern Vietnam through the country's rural areas, ethnic minority areas, and ancient capital of Hue to the southern extremity in the Mekong delta. Many of the songs draw from indigenous material such as regional styles and pentatonic melodies performed in a style known as *tân nhạc*, a modern popular fusion of Western instrumentation and orchestration. The result is a symbolic call for national unity (with important modern and ancient components), celebrating regional difference and cultural diversity and a protest against the Geneva Convention's (1954) division of Vietnam into separate North and South political entities.

In contrast to the government condemnation of Phạm Duy, the communist government heartily endorsed many compositions by Văn Cao. His heroic love songs in particular were a major inspiration for popular singers and songwriters throughout the post war period. I have already introduced you to his song "Tien quan ca" (Onward Soldiers) that was selected for the national anthem in 1976 (see pg. 100).

Arguably the most celebrated composer/songwriter in 20th century Vietnam is Trịnh Công Sơn. Born in central Vietnam in 1939 Trịnh Công Sơn wrote over six hundred songs. Many of his songs of the 1960s and 70s had a distinctly anti-war flavor. Sơn's pacifist lyrics were said to destroy the will to fight and his meditations on fate, informed by Vietnamese Buddhism, encouraged a degree of mistrust by the country's leaders. His pacifist and critical lyrics led to songs occasionally being restricted by the South Vietnamese government (pre-1975) and then to his imprisonment in re-education camps after the fall of Saigon and the reunification of Vietnam. After the war his love songs and appeals to national postwar reconciliation earned even greater popularity, although the Vietnamese government continued to intermittently suppress his music. His protest songs garnered international attention during the war and he was dubbed the Bob Dylan of Vietnam by Joan Baez—a term that stayed with his international reputation until his death in 2001.

Through his songs, Sơn earned a reputation of serving general humanist goals rather than narrow political ones, writing works "in which he opposed hatred and killing irrespective of what side the haters and killers were on" (Schafer 2007: 632). For example, "A Lullaby of Cannons for the Night" (Đại Bác Ru Đêm) paints a mournful picture of a mother comforting her child who falls asleep each night to cannon fire. Hints of Buddhist and nationalist sentiment are found woven through a humanist anti-war appeal. Nationalist sentiment in Trịnh Công Sơn's music is not patriotic but rather an appeal to a common humanity and to shared land—quite distinct from the patriotic national unification agendas of a government. Readers are encouraged to visit the Vietnamese music database <www. vmdb.com> to explore this and other Trịnh Công Sơn songs.

A Lullaby of Cannons for the Night (excerpt)
Every night cannon shells create a future without life
Cannons like a chant without a prayer
Children forget to live and anxiously wait.

Every night cannons resound in the town
A street cleaner stops sweeping and listens

Every night cannons sing a lullaby for golden skin
The cannons sound like a prelude to a familiar sad song
And children are gone before they see their native land
Words and music by Trịnh Công Sơn; translated
by Cao Thị Như-Quỳnh and John C. Schafer
(quoted in Schafer 2007)

Through the decades after the war Vietnamese popular music was increasingly influenced by foreign styles—especially after the country's embrace of capitalism, the 1985 national renovation (đổi mới) policies and the 1994 lifting of the U.S. trade embargo by President Clinton. Trịnh Công Sơn's music remains very popular among Vietnamese today. Though he had endured a career of critique from the communist government, his official recognition by the state at his funeral in 2001 seemed to forget many of his "misdeeds"—another example of the selective remembering (and forgetting) of official state history. Hundreds of thousands of people gathered at his funeral for a spontaneous concert in Ho Chi Minh City; it was one of the largest funeral processions in Vietnamese history, second only to Hồ Chí Minh's.

Cambodia. Cambodia's recent history offers us a different perspective from which to examine the relationships between music and political turmoil. The Cambodian genocide (1975–79) unleashed unspeakable horrors on the people of Cambodia. Close to two million people were killed during this period through the policies of Pol Pot and the Communist Party of Kampuchea (the Khmer Rouge). The revolution's leadership, known by the appellation of Angkar, or "organization," strove to be the sole focus of people's loyalties. The regime romanticized agrarianism, forcing urban populations out of the cities and into rural labor camps where they were to become "new people." Policies of mass relocation and family separation tore people from their communities. Millions died from starvation, disease, torture, and execution in less than four years of Angkar rule. Religious worship, markets and free association were banned. Those with an education, upper-class status, or religious affiliation were particularly vulnerable to this "great leap" toward a self-reliant, agrarian, socialist state. Even something as simple as wearing glasses, interpreted as a symbol of education and elite status, would warrant persecution.

Music as a concept was not outlawed, but its associations, uses, and functions were highly suspect. All musics, dance, and other arts during Angkar rule were to serve the state ideology: anything that didn't serve this purpose was banned. A Khmer Rouge notebook from the 1970s lists "Contemporary Principles of Cultural Politics" in which it is noted that "every kind of art production among the masses is intended to wipe out the enemy's art(s) and to build new art(s) [and to] serve the people's art to the extent possible" (quoted in Shapiro-Phim 2002: 181). They forbade a wide variety of dance and music and allowed no performance of pre-revolutionary popular, folk, or ritual songs. Classical music and dance relating to the royal court, foreign musics, and Buddhist chant were all inappropriate. Cambodia's traditional and contemporary arts of almost all forms stopped. As a result many practitioners of these traditions were killed or were forced to suppress their knowledge.

Khmer Rouge leaders did recognize the power of song and dance to signify particular social ideologies. They created displays of revolutionary songs and dances through which they redefined reality and indoctrinated the masses with Angkar loyalty and a stifling social-ist ideology. The calendar was reset to year 0—no class divisions, no money, no books, no schools, no hospitals.

Arn Chorn-Pond was a child when the Khmer Rouge took over Cambodia. While 90% of the country's musicians were killed or starved, some people in fact were spared for their musical ability and were forced to play propaganda songs for the Khmer Rouge soldiers. Arn Chorn-Pond's flute playing saved him from death but drove him into a psychological hell as he was forced to facilitate the murders commit-ted by the soldiers. Eventually escaping the "killing fields," he found his way to a refugee camp in Thailand where an American missionary adopted him.

Jocelyn Glatzer's film *The Flute Player* (Figure 4.3) begins more than twenty years later in Lowell, Massachusetts, where Arn Chorn-Pond works with Cambodian-American youth, teaching them Khmer tra-ditional musics and encouraging them to compose and reflect musically on their own lives. This moving film follows Arn from Massachusetts back to Cambodia, as he seeks out senior master musicians who survived

FIGURE 4.3 *The Flute Player. Arn Chorn-Pond at Cheung Ek Killing Fields Memorial.* *(Photo credit: Sonith Heng.)*

the Khmer Rouge regime. Arn manages to find numerous master folk and classical musicians, records their music and, effectively, re-starts many of their careers.

To seek out surviving musicians, Arn Chorn-Pond founded the "Cambodian Masters Performing Project" now named "Cambodian Living Arts." Many of these master artists, successful singers or popular artists before the Khmer Rouge, were found living in abject poverty and, of necessity, had been forced to deny their musical identities. One artist, Master Kong Nai, a singer and performer of the *chapei* (a long-necked lute), has, since becoming involved in this project, received significant attention, performing for the Smithsonian World Arts festival and recently recording an album under Peter Gabriel's Real World label (CD track 23).

ACTIVITY 4.7   *Listen to Kong Nai play "Farewell Wishes" on CD track 25.*

On subsequent listenings pay particular attention to the following:

The pitches. Notice the tunings of some of the pitches and how they differ from a Western scale. Return to CD track 12 (the Khmer pinn peat ensemble). Note the similarities in the scale.

Focus more intently now on the relationship between the voice and the chapei. Note the activity on the chapei when the Kong Nai is not singing and its relative stasis when he is singing.

Lastly, listen for the ornamentation (particularly on long-held notes) on both the chapei and the voice. How does the quavering vibrato of the voice get "imitated" on the chapei?

The Cambodian Living Arts project has sponsored many elder musicians who survived the Pol Pot era, but it has also moved beyond salvage ethnomusicology that seeks to "save" or "recover" a tradition. The organization's name change from the "Cambodian Master Performers Project" to "Cambodian Living Arts" speaks to this. In addition to documenting traditional arts it also sponsors new works and contemporary projects, some of which I will discuss further in Chapter 5. The mission of the organization is to change the international perception of the country, hoping that Cambodia will someday be known not for the killing fields but for its thriving arts and culture.

ACTIVITY 4.8 *The website for Cambodian Living Arts is a valuable place to learn more about Cambodian music. The website includes brief biographies and performances by several master musicians (Nong Chock, Youn Mec, and Yim Saing) and provides fascinating glimpses of musical survival. It also includes interviews with Arn Chorn-Pond, descriptions of Cambodian traditional instruments and ensembles (such as the* chapei *and those discussed in Chapter 2), and recorded samples of traditional and new compositions.*

Visit the website for Cambodian Living Arts <http://www.cambodianlivingarts.org>

Make note of the wide variety of artistic endeavors promoted through this organization.

Discuss among your classmates the following: How might one determine whether a project like Cambodian Living Arts is successful?

While the cultural preservation project and the stories of elder musicians drives much of the film, a crucial second theme in *The Flute Player* is Arn Chorn-Pond himself, as he confronts many of the demons from his own past. When the Vietnamese invaded in 1979, after almost four years of Angkar rule, Arn, still only 14 years old, was given an AK-47 and told to fight. Shortly thereafter, Arn fled, eventually reaching Thailand. This film is a testament to his ongoing quest to transcend this heartbreaking catastrophe.

ACTIVITY 4.9 *A. If you can get a hold of the film* The Flute Player, *watch it and prepare to discuss each of these questions with a classmate.*

What moments in the film had an emotional impact for you? Why?

To what scenes can you point that best help you understand Arn Chorn-Pond's motivation to create the Master Performers project?

Reflect on the scene between Arn and the former soldier sharing their "guilt". To what degree is each of them responsible for the Cambodian genocide?

Take particular note of the way that music is intertwined throughout the story. In what specific ways does music both facilitate the genocide and the recovery from the genocide?

Visit the PBS website for the film www.pbs.org/pov/pov2003/ thefluteplayer to facilitate your discussion.

B. If you have access to it and enjoy learning through literature I recommend that you also explore Music Through the Dark, *a short biography of Cambodian accordionist Daran Kravanh's experiences surviving the Khmer Rouge (see additional resources). This will permit you to compare Daran Kravanh's experiences with those of Arn Chorn Pond's.*

Burma/Myanmar. In September of 2007 Buddhist monks took to the streets throughout Burma/Myanmar to protest a variety of oppressive government policies. An unannounced increase in gas prices (ranging from 200%–500%) on August 15th was the primary catalyst for the demonstrations, though the conditions were ripe for such an explosion (as explained in Chapter 1). As with many types of civil disobedience, music played a significant role in protests both in real time and on the Internet in the months following the event.

The Saffron Revolution of September 2007 presents competing visions of authority between the *sangha* (the order of monks) and the military government, that is, between Buddhist law (*vinaya*) and secular law. Political engagement by monks is regarded by many people as problematic and fundamentally at odds with the spiritual role of the *sangha*. For some, monks are supposed to be above the concerns of our mundane political lives and devoted instead to more fundamental problems of *dhamma* (Buddhist teaching). To concern themselves with worldly politics is to show attachment. Such a simple reading denies the symbiotic relationship between the *sangha* and the laity, however.

During the revolution and also in preceding political uprisings dating to the colonial period, monks employed two important symbols rooted in *vinaya* (Buddhist law and practice): *pattam* or turning over the alms bowl, and chanting of the *Metta Sutta*. These symbols are rooted in the social relationship between the *sangha* and the public.

Political engagement by the monks is dependent on a subversion of the relationship between the *sangha* and the rulers. As mentioned in the first chapter, one of the primary social roles of the *sangha* is to be a "field of merit"—a conduit through which the laity (including government/ military personnel) may make merit. By donating to monks and to monasteries (a daily cultural practice in Myanmar), the laity earns karmic merit. This practice of *dana*, a ritual exchange of giving, earns merit, cultivates generosity and is ultimately intended to destroy the impulse that leads to attachment and to further suffering. The donor (of food, robes, shelter, etc.) not only earns *kammic* (karmic) merit but also an increase in social and political status. Buddhism here is overtly political based upon an economy of merit.

In early September, as the revolution was beginning, a clash between monks and military police resulted in some physical assaults on monks. When apologies for the attacks on monks were not forthcoming the *sangha* at large turned over their alms bowls and invoked a ritual called *pattam*. According to *pattam*, monks can boycott any persons engaging in behavior out of line with Buddhism or regarded as inhumane. Monks can shun these people by not accepting religious offerings from them or not helping them to perform religious ceremonies. These persons can be boycotted until they make an apology. By refusing donations, the monks negate the status and the legitimacy of the rulers and the conflict between Buddhist law and secular law is driven to the surface. This has happened several times in Burma's past—always at socially heightened moments.

At many of their gathering places both on the street and at Buddhist pagodas the monks engaged a second example of political theater by chanting the *Metta Sutta* (CD track 24). Metta, often translated from the Pali language as "loving-kindness," is one of four mental states that Buddhist practice aims to cultivate (the others being compassion, sympathetic joy, and equanimity). The *Metta Sutta* was taught by the Buddha to a group of forest monks who were disturbed by tree spirits. He urged them to practice loving-kindness towards all beings. The practice of loving kindness resolved the fear and conflict and appeased the aggressive forces. Over the years the Metta Sutta has become emblematic of social engagement and has recently developed a strong association with the democracy movement. Important here is the performed assertion that democracy is in line with Buddhist law.

Mettā Sutta

1. Karaṇīyamattha-kusalena
  Yantaṃ santaṃ padaṃ
    abhisamecca
  Sakko ujū ca sūjū ca
  Suvaco cassa mudu anatimānī
	1. Let no one deceive another
	  Nor despise any person
	    whatever in any place,
	  Either in anger or in ill will,
	  Let one not wish any harm
	    to another.

2. Santussako ca subharo ca
 	
  Appakicco ca sallahukavutti
  Santindriyo ca nipako ca
  Appagabbho kulesu
    ananugiddho
	2. Just as a mother would
	    protect her only child
	  Even at her own life's risk,
	  So let him cultivate
	  A boundless heart towards all
	    beings.

3. Na ca khuddaṃ samācare kiñci
  Yena viññū pare upavadeyyum
 	
  Sukhino vā khemino hontu!
 	
  Sabbe sattā bhavantu sukhitattā!
	3. Let his heart of boundless love
	  Pervade the whole world
	    above,
	  Below and across; with no
	    obstruction,
	  No hatred and no enmity.

(Vandanā: The Album of Pāḷi Devotional Chanting & Hymns: 2002)

ACTIVITY 4.10   *Find online a copy of the entire Metta Sutta text.*

  Listen to the Metta Sutta being recited as a prayer or a meditation and reflect on what the meaning of the words might be to the practitioner.

  Listen carefully to CD track 24 (and other versions that you have found online, recall the source <http://www.buddhanet.net/audio.htm>). Note the musical approach to the text and how it prioritizes articulation and clarity of the text.

On September 21st, the monks marched to the home of Aung San Suu Kyi (recall Figure 4.2). Suu Kyi, the Nobel Peace Prize laureate whose party won an election in 1990 but was never allowed to take office, has been under house arrest for thirteen of the last eighteen years. Since her latest detention began in May 2003 she has rarely been allowed to see visitors outside her gated, guarded compound in Yangon. Monks arrived at the gate of her home and again chanted the *Metta Sutta*, the Buddha's discourse on loving-kindness. Neither the public nor the press had seen Aung San Suu Kyi in over three years. Opening her gate, Suu Kyi acknowledged the monks and accepted the blessing of the *Metta Sutta*. Theatrically and sonically the relationship between democracy and Buddhist law was performed and, more specifically, a relationship was articulated between the *sangha* and the one who they regarded as the appropriate ruler/leader.

While there had been numerous small violent skirmishes in various parts of the country the revolution up to this point had been relatively peaceful though quite tense, and the key protest strategies employed (*pattam* and chanting the *Metta Sutta*) had been explicitly non-violent. The intensity of the protests peaked in the third week of September when gunfire, teargas volleys, sirens, and beatings interrupted the sound of the *Metta Sutta*. Loudspeakers announcing night curfews and raids upon various monasteries stretched into the night. Arrests of several thousand monks were made and the estimates of those killed in the crackdown range from 31 to 300; it is a number we will never know.

As the *sangha* is essential to Burmese culture at large (and political legitimacy of any ruler) one of the first things the military did upon arresting the monks was to disrobe them and assert publicly that these were rogue monks—not true monks—and that their conduct was not monk-like. They had transgressed *vinaya* (Buddhist law). The monks in turn replied with a different interpretation of Buddhist law, asserting that the refusal to accept donations does not constitute a violent act in itself.

ACTIVITY 4.11   *Search the Internet for photos of the Saffron Revolution. Reflect on the relationship between the visual images and the sounds discussed above.*

Politically engaged Buddhism has a long history in Burma/Myanmar and was central to the country's independence movement. The monks U Ottama and U Wisara are national heroes for their willingness in the 1930s to take on sacrifice (and subject themselves to violence) for progressive social ends. Politically engaged monks today employ ritual sounds to serve political ends.

CONCLUSION

In contrast to many perceptions of musical activity, it is not always a pacifier, a source of comfort or solace. Despite William Congreve's lines "music hath charms to soothe a savage breast, to soften rocks, or bend a knotted oak," we can also find in music the power to inflame the savage, harden attitudes, and stiffen resolve. Music is often involved in political strife and rarely in a neutral way. There is no shortage of political contexts in which we can find music playing an active role in resolving or inflaming conflict. For this reason, in a discussion of music and politics it is worthwhile to be reminded that music can be used for harm as well as for good.

This chapter has been organized in two basic parts: firstly, I have discussed several top down efforts by governments trying to organize music for particular state endorsed ends. Administrators or politicians can sanction musical activities and projects, as they recognize that music helps shape ideas such as the nation. National schools, notations, and other forms of standardization often result. In contrast, other musico-political behavior can be found on a more grassroots level, as people react to various policies, injustices, or overtures by government forces. These conflicts between people and their governments may play out in numerous ways as ethnicity, religion, regionality, or any number of other social identity markers contribute to how the conflict is understood.

Many of these conflicts and the musical means for commenting on them take on a global character or are increasingly influenced by the sounds, distribution, and marketing forces of the global economy. The musical resources available to a political body—both in terms of sonic materials and distribution—are rapidly expanding and quickly changing the style, and meanings, of many conflicts. Recognizing the influence of foreign sounds and ideas I turn your attention now to the influence of globalization on music and musical practice in mainland Southeast Asia. Some claim that the power of globalization is so significant that the role of the nation-state is in decline and that the nation-state is no longer the primary agent in determining a local culture or a cultural identity. Yet, this chapter has given some evidence of cases to the contrary, where national and local authorities incorporate global trends or ideas and use them to shape a distinct local culture. To these contrary forces—the local and the global—we will now turn.

CHAPTER 5

Globalization and Local Adaptation

GLOBALIZATION

What is globalization and why is it talked about as something new? Mass migrations from the north over two thousand years ago, long exchanges with China and India over several millennia, interactions with Western colonial forces over the past two centuries, and a present-day digital connection with the global community: it is clear that mainland Southeast Asia has never been isolated. The flow of resources, ideas, and people across borders has had regular and changing influences on economic, political, and cultural systems throughout the region (see Fig 5.1).

Though communities, nations, and empires have always been interacting with their neighbors, few would dispute the fact that the pace of change and the range of influences upon these societies have increased dramatically since World War II and especially in the last two decades of the 20th century. In many respects, while globalization is not necessarily new, the globalization and modernizing forces of today are significantly different than global trends one hundred years ago. The past decades have fueled a growing awareness among people of the relationships between the local and the distant, between their community and communities elsewhere on the planet. These relationships are realized through a multidimensional set of social processes and exchanges that "create, multiply, stretch, and intensify worldwide social interdependencies" (Steger 2003: 13).

Such processes have had significant influence on the music cultures of mainland Southeast Asia for both the benefit and detriment of musical traditions. Shifting forms of human contact have led to much greater degrees of integration and interdependence. Musics tied most closely to lifestyles impacted by changing relationships are inevitably, and quite naturally, the most likely to change or to completely disappear.

FIGURE 5.1 *Mac Burger: While economic sanctions forbid American companies from doing business in Burma/Myanmar, global images and ideas still circulate. Mac Burger, in downtown Rangoon, hosts a large golden M on its window, serves bland hamburgers, and has a scary clown for a mascot.*

Mechanization of agricultural practices, for example, may result in the loss of songs that once accompanied the planting, transplanting, threshing, and husking of rice. If a machine can do the work then work songs designed to regulate rhythm, as well as pass the time for the human worker, will disappear or possibly be recontextualized with new altered meanings in a new setting. Changes in farming practices may also force people out of the rural areas and into the cities to look for work, leading to larger cities and a change of demographics within both urban and rural areas. Songs and dances brought to the cities by villagers may possibly be no longer useful or may find new life as the people change and adapt to the new urban environment. That same worker may return to the village and, in addition to hard-earned money, may bring back new musical ideas, recordings, or instruments to be recontextualized in the village.

This simple abstract example highlights several important issues surrounding the process of globalization. Firstly, while many traditional life-ways and musical contexts may be lost to these changes, globalization also leads to the creation of new (and multiple) social networks and, thus, musical contexts and behaviors. Secondly, the social relationships of many of these migrants have been accelerated, intensified, and stretched. Lastly, the social connections and interdependencies have not only been accelerated and magnified objectively (i.e., more types of relationships, more access to a variety of ideas and goods) but on a conscious level people are increasingly aware of their relations with people elsewhere in the world.

Some theorists of globalization claim that increased and accelerated interdependencies of economies, political systems, and cultures are eroding our national boundaries. Such theories assert that political power, economic sway, and cultural influence is located in global social formations and distributed through global networks (media, financial, political) rather than through territorially based states and their governments. In essence, the nation-state is no longer a central force in the formation of cultural identity.

In contrast, other theorists argue that the growing interconnectedness of communities has facilitated the mobilization of political power on the local level. Communities in specific locales now have access to cultural (political, economic, media, etc.) resources—forged through these interconnections—through which they can assert their own local identities and define themselves vis-à-vis other locales, countries, religions, etc. Such claims assert that local communities still matter very much.

In music scholarship, these two poles of thought have been debated at length for several decades. In the 1960s folklorist/ethnomusicologist Alan Lomax warned of "cultural grey-out," adopting the view that globalization causes musical forms to acculturate to the mainstream status-quo and become homogenized—with the English language music industry dominant. Other, more recent studies argue the opposite: that population mobility and technology facilitates the creation of new musical forms.

ACTIVITY 5.1 *Cultural grey-out or increased local diversity?*
Based on material thus far discussed, choose a position and prepare for a debate with your classmates. Choose whether you want to take the position that musical forms, contexts, and behaviors have homogenized and have lost uniqueness in the face of

*globalization. Or choose to point to local manifestations of differ-
ence and self-determined cultural identity facilitated by the process
of globalization. Develop 6–8 examples to support your argu-
ment and spend some time anticipating the opinions counter to
your position.*

A study of contemporary music traditions in mainland Southeast
Asia, then, demands acknowledgement of both these powerful homogenizing forces and of the tendencies to localize meaning. The resulting
hybridity of styles and contexts is not simply a matter of similarity or
difference. Cultural globalization—the symbolic creation, performance,
articulation and distribution of meaning—always takes place in local
contexts. The combination of the local and the global in some current
scholarship rejects both cultural homogenization and local autonomy
and speaks instead of glocalization, the adoption of a foreign product
into a specific local (see Stokes 2004).

Closer analysis of cultural change throughout Southeast Asia shows
us that globalization is not an even process. It does not happen uniformly at the same rate and with the same impact across the region but,
rather, is a very uneven process that impacts some people and communities significantly while leaving others relatively untouched. In addition, some communities may change radically in specific areas through
some aspects of the global process and other cultural patterns in those
same communities remain unchanged. In Laos and Cambodia, where
survival and rejuvenation (resuscitation) of the tradition is primary,
innovation takes a secondary position and may be more difficult to find
(revisit CD track 21 and 23). Myanmar and Thailand, on the other hand,
have vibrant traditions that (despite radically different political situations) foster regular musical innovation (revisit the music by the King of
Thailand (Activity 4.3), and listen to CD tracks 26, 27, 28, to be discussed
shortly). Again, however, musical life in all of these societies resists
broad sweeping generalizations. Think of the Cambodian Living Arts
Project discussed in Chapter 4 and again below: it is simultaneously a
catalyst for preservation AND for innovation.

Musical innovation is most obvious in cases where foreign instruments are used or combined with indigenous instruments (see CD track
26, 27, 28, 29 below) but could also be identified through changes of context (concert hall, online, etc.), distribution (printed notation, digital file

swapping, etc), or other manipulators of meaning. Outsiders (or even locals unfamiliar with traditional musics) often label "traditional" modern musical compositions that hold to traditional instrumentation, as in modern compositions for *piphat* or *saing waing* ensemble. Examples of compositional innovation are also unevenly distributed across the region. Urban centers may offer more examples of new composition than the rural areas.

WESTERN CONCEPTIONS AND STEREOTYPES

Another tool for understanding the exchange of culture is through film. American musicians and filmmakers have used Southeast Asia as a platform through which to make a comment or critique of American values to help define what it means to be American. For much of the past few decades association to Cambodia and Burma found in American music would conjure up the 1980s punk bands *Mission of Burma* and the Dead Kennedys with their song "Holiday in Cambodia." Both of these punk bands used titular images of Southeast Asia to offer commentary on American lifestyles. They don't actually have much to say about Burma or Cambodia but offer significant commentary on America: using the Other to make a comment on their own community. American protest music of the 1960s and 1970s turned Vietnam from a country to a war. As I have mentioned, even today an Internet search of "Vietnam and music" will draw a majority of American made songs for American audiences (a cautionary tale for Internet research). Indeed, identity (ethnic, national, gender, etc) is defined in relation to and often through some other. These references to Southeast Asian countries surely say much more about America than they do about Southeast Asia. How, though, does this construction of American identity forged through foreign textual, visual, musical, and filmic images contribute to stereotypes or understandings of Southeast Asian culture?

ACTIVITY 5.2   *How do American understandings of Southeast Asia continue to circulate? How is Southeast Asia continually used to build "American" or "British" identities?*

View a Western film that is based in Southeast Asia, from the following list.

Forrest Gump, Full Metal Jacket, Apocalypse Now, We Were Soldiers, Platoon, The Killing Fields, Bridge on the River Kwai, Objective Burma, Indochine, Good Morning Vietnam, The Lover, Born on the Fourth of July, The Deer Hunter, Beyond Rangoon, Rambo IV, The King and I/Anna and the King, The Beach, City of Ghosts.
How are the locals depicted in these films?
What musical elements are used to depict local scenes or people?
How do these films help to create a sense of Americanness or Britishness? How do they sculpt Thai-ness, Khmer-ness, etc.?
Revisit activity 1.1 or do it again. Think about the images and stereotypes of Southeast Asia that have entered through these movies. Discuss these images with your classmates.

THE LONG HISTORY OF GLOBALIZATION

As you now know, mainland Southeast Asia has been greatly influenced by foreign peoples for millennia. Travelers from India had major influences on Southeast Asia in the form of the Khmer languages, various writing systems, Hinduism, Theravada Buddhism (and their related concepts such as the god-king), sculpture, musical instruments (drums, harps and oboes), narratives such as the Ramayana and Mahabharata, dance dramas, mudras, rasa, poetry, and cyclical notions of time (revisit Chapter 1, for review). Chinese civilization brought different cuisines, Mahayana Buddhism, musical instruments (zithers, drums, two string bowed lutes) and different types of theater (see Chapter 2).

The Burmese in Ayutthaya. Musical exchange between kingdoms internal to the region is also apparent. Political expansion and warfare has led to increased exchange brought on by the migration of people (both forced and unforced). As I have mentioned, in 1767, the Burmese empire under King Hsinbyushin attacked the Siamese capital Ayutthaya. Villages were burned to the ground and few buildings survived (Figure 5.2); even Buddhist temples and pagodas were destroyed. Still a sore point, the death and destruction wrought from this attack is remembered and reconstructed in big-budget Thai films such as *Bang*

FIGURE 5.2   *Ruins of Ayutthaya.*

Rajan (2000) and *Suriyothai* (2001). Several Thai I spoke with in Ayutthaya spoke of Burmese marauders as if the attacks were very recent; even many Burmese today are embarrassed by the needless destruction of the Thai capital.

Having conquered Ayutthaya and extended the reach of the Konbaung dynasty the Burmese military returned to the Burmese capital of Ava with thousands of Thai artists, artisans, dancers, and carvers. One of the most famous Burmese composers and poets, Mya-wadi U Sa (1766–1853) was charged by the crown prince to translate and adapt for the Burmese stage the Siamese version of the Ramayana (see Williamson 1979). The great Hindu epic, the Ramayana, is found in the Khmer kingdom by the 6th C (C.E.) where it is called the *Reamker* and in the Sukothai kingdom of Thailand by the 13th C (C.E.), known there as the *Ramakien*. The Indian influence is clearly found through the presence of the Ramayana epic but both the *Reamker* and the *Ramakien* would barely be recognized back in India. Burma/Myanmar's version, the *Yamayana*, is largely drawn from the Ayutthaya prisoners of war. Many other Siamese-style songs were adapted into Burmese court music, translated orally from the aging Siamese royal musician-hostages who never returned to Ayutthaya. A famous genre of classical pieces called *Yodaya thachin* (Yodaya songs, from the Burmese word for Thailand) is—even today—a major staple of the Burmese Thachin' Gyi (Great Song) repertoire. One of the most famous pieces is "Myaman Giri." You have already heard "Myanman Giri" on CD track 10 played on the bamboo xylophone, *pattala* (see Figure 2.8).

Modernizing Thailand.   Southeast Asia struggled to negotiate French and British forces throughout the 19th century. Much of the reason for Thailand not falling under colonial power lay in how Thailand wrestled with the forces of modernization. As Western economic, political, and cultural forces swept through the peninsula throughout the 19th century, countries/kingships struggled to reconcile their traditions with the inevitable forces of modernization. The process of classicization discussed in Chapter 4 was one manifestation of this process.

To embrace modernization and not equate it to Westernization was a significant struggle for King Mongkut (1851–1868) and his son Chulalongkorn (1868–1910) in Siam. Today King Mongkut (Rama IV) is recognized in Thailand as the "Father of Modern Science and Technology." Acutely aware of the growing threat from British and French powers, he studied much Western science, including astronomy, Latin and English and began to implement practices of Western medicine. He established a free (non-governmental) newspaper and ordered his nobility to wear shirts while attending his court. He hired numerous foreign instructors to teach his 39 wives and 82 children.

One of these instructors, Anna Leonowens, provoked great debate and is still the subject of controversy. Her experiences were recorded (and fictionalized) in Margaret Landon's 1944 novel *Anna and the King of Siam*, which was later translated into a highly successful Rogers and Hammerstein musical comedy, *The King and I* (1951), and several feature length films. Anna Leonowens served at the Siamese court for six years as teacher and English-language secretary to the king. Shortly after she returned to England (with plans to come back to Siam), Mongkut passed away and fifteen-year old Chulalongkorn became the new monarch. Continuing his father's modernizing interests, Chulalongkorn implemented further reforms, several of which Leonowens claimed credit for. It is still debated how much influence Leonowens had on the young prince. Given Siam/Thailand's efforts to not be regarded as "child-like" barbarians that needed Western tutelage, the story of Anna and the King has become a point of contention throughout the past 60 years (see Morgan 2008).

The book, the musical, and numerous films (all based on the experiences of Leonowens) have had significant longevity for Western audiences and have continued to portray in a controversial light Thailand's relationship to the West at a pivotal time in its history. In Thailand today the fictional depiction of the king is condemned as heretical and disrespectful. For this reason, the Rodgers and Hammerstein film, along with the 1999 remake filmed in Malaysia starring American actor Jodie Foster and Chinese actor Chow Yun-Fat, remains officially banned.

ACTIVITY 5.3 *Watch the 1954 film* The King and I *(with Deborah Kerr and Yul Brenner) and/or the 1999 film (with Jodie Foster and Chow Yun-Fat). Or for a bigger project include the 1946 film* Anna and the King of Siam *with Rex Harrison and Irene Dunne (and Balinese rather than Thai music!).*

Prepare to discuss these questions with classmates:

What role does music and dance (Thai and Western) play in establishing the characters and advancing the story?

What does the movie say about the relationship between Thailand and the West? What problems are there in this depiction?

What does the 1999 film say through its production values and its choice of actors about Thailand's contemporary relationship to the United States and China?

If you can watch both films, what significant changes are there between 1954 and 1999 in the representation of Thailand?

Chulalongkorn was well aware of how disparagingly Siam was viewed by the West and struggled with the apparent contradictions of modernism and tradition. On his visit to Europe in 1897 he was struck by the unevenness of European modernity—the glaring inequalities of this "new" system. Chulalongkorn learned the difference between Westernization and modernization. Only modernization could permit the survival of a Thai national identity. "I am convinced," he said upon his return, "there exists no incompatibility between [the acquisition of European science] and the maintenance of our individuality as an independent Asiatic nation" (*The Bangkok Times*, 26 Jan. 1898, Quoted in Wyatt 2003: 197).

Chulalongkorn brought sweeping changes and strong leadership into the 20th century. At this time, with Burma a colony of Britain and Cambodia and Vietnam under French control, Western commercial demand for facilities and security was a pressing concern for the King. The urgency to modernize or face colonization was palpable. The most serious need was for a reform in education (Wyatt 2003), as he realized that education was a prerequisite for political, economic, and social development—especially for civil servants who would need some understanding of the changes to come.

The young King Chulalongkorn did modernize the Siamese government in numerous ways, not the least of which was abandoning the semi-feudal administrations to a modern one of provinces and districts. He traveled to neighboring European colonies, studied European and American politics, administration, and lifestyle. He was the first Thai king to visit Europe, opened the first railroad (from Bangkok to Ayutthaya in 1896), replaced the traditional lunar calendar with the Western calendar, introduced modern banknotes, and declared religious freedom (in a predominantly Buddhist country), allowing greater opportunities to Christian and Islamic communities. Such activities garnered him the title "The Great Beloved King"; he is generally regarded as one of Thailand's greatest kings.

> **ACTIVITY 5.4** *Reflect further on the Thai film* The Overture *that you watched for activity 4.4.*
>
> *The film dramatizes the conflicts inherent in the musical "modernization" of Thailand shortly after Chulalongkorn's reign.*
>
> *What significant differences are noticeable in the depictions of Thai culture as compared to* Anna and the King?

French-Influenced Vietnam. Impressed by Chinese theater for hundreds of years, the early 20th century saw a gradual increase in French influence on Vietnamese traditions and somewhat less cultural dominance from China. In 1913, a romanized version of the Vietnamese script became the official writing system and Chinese characters fell into disuse. French colonists had introduced many European instruments to Vietnam as well as styles of music associated with military and religious (Roman Catholic) contexts. The Catholic Church and military bands served as a training ground for many Vietnamese composers and performers learning Western compositional methods and instruments respectively. After WWI French popular songs became increasingly popular in the urban areas due to the spread of sound recording technology particularly 78 r.p.m recordings and radio. Other strong French influences of the 1920s and 30s included ballroom dancing and "talkies," sound motion pictures. Many pieces associated with these diverse contexts found their way into popular *cải lương* theater (see Gibbs 1988).

Cải lương (reformed theater) developed from a combination of classical theater (*hát bội*) and instrumental not-for-profit music making of southern Vietnam (*tài tử*) at the beginning of the 20th century, combining Vietnamese songs and French music and a conscious withdrawl from Chinese melodies. *Tài tử* music consists only of chordophones (*đàn tranh*, zither [Figure 2.15, CD track 15]; *đàn cơ* or *đàn nhị*, bowed lute and *đàn kìm*, dulcimer), and one small idiophone (the *song lang* clapper) though the ensemble is not standardized. In *tài tử* music the instrumentalists played a role equal to that of the singers and, in keeping with its urban, cosmopolitan audience and context, frequently incorporated modified European instruments such as the guitar, the fiddle, and the steel guitar as heard on CD track 16. Unlike traditional *hát bội* theater, which used predominantly Vietnamese and Chinese stories, *cải lương* modified legends, histories, stories, and satires from many additional countries—France, Egypt, Japan, and others—significantly stretching its source material. It also drew from Western operatic traditions (learned from colonial opera houses) in its use of set decoration, scenery, and a full combination of acting dancing, singing, and mime. The emphasis, however, was consistently upon song and the seemless flow between the 7-tone speech of the Vietnamese language and song articulated in the vernacular language of the people (Nguyen 2008, 276).

Extending the globalizing music culture of Vietnam—already well under way through military and Roman Catholic musical influences—*cải lương* was a significant player in the modernist movement of the early 1900s. Because of its origins in Southern Vietnam *cải lương* can be found today practiced among the Vietnamese diaspora community of the United States (see Nguyen 2003).

ACTIVITY 5.5 *Listen to CD track 16.*
Pay attention to the relationship between speech and voice.
Notice the emphasis on string instruments. Alternately focus
on the modified guitar (see CD track 29 below) and the bowed
lute đàn cơ *or* đàn nịh.

Music Notation and Globalization. The globalization process can also be examined through the adoption and use of music notation in these countries. Rote memorization of pieces is still the preferred method of transmission for traditional musics throughout Southeast Asia. Teachers play the first phrase of a piece for a student who is then required to play it back. Only when the student has the phrase committed to memory would the teacher move on to the second phrase. Oral transmission of this kind is difficult and time intensive for both teacher and student. Years of study lead to vast mental stores of memorized pieces and the ability to call them up spontaneously. As one way of testing the level of my musicianship, I was frequently asked how many songs I knew. To know a piece is to have it memorized. If I had learned the piece, transcribed it and yet not committed it to memory, I did not know it. If I replied that I knew five to ten pieces by memory on the *hne* (Fig. 2.3, CD track 8) then I was clearly (and rightly) regarded as a beginner.

Memorization of the tradition has been a mark of authority. Recall the Mingun Sayadaw U Vicittasarabivamsa that I referred to in Chapter 1. This famous monk was revered for his memorization of the entire *Tripitika* (approximately 50 volumes) and his ability to recall obscure passages spontaneously. To be sure, the use of musical notation—the (usually) written representation of musical sounds—is more the exception than the rule in Southeast Asia.

However, the introduction over the past century of different notation systems and the "foreign" concepts of preservation and standardization have had significant influence on music practice and provide another interesting example of early 20th century globalization trends. The concept of a static unchanging piece, as would be implied by a notated script of a piece, is a relatively new concept in this region. The notion that music must be preserved and documented lest it die out appears to indicate, as Thai music scholar Pamela Moro notes, "an altered perception of time, change, and the fixedness of music itself (that is, that a piece of music should be fixed at all rather than mutating through individual innovations over time); this may well have come from the West, where we have written down compositions for a long time" (Myers-Moro 1993: 146). They further reveal an increased degree of reflexivity—making note of and documenting culture, as the prospects for change loom ever greater.

In Chapter 4, I spoke of the role that notation systems have had in the codification (cataloging, organizing, and historicizing) of a nation's music, and the role that notations play in political assertions of the nation. I now return to the concept of notation as an example of the globalization of particular musical behaviors (transmission, preservation) and concepts. In some traditions oral transmission may lead to great variation from performance to performance and differences from one teacher to another may be vast. Indeed the differences between one master's version and another are a fundamental element of musical style and authority. Particularly in contexts where instrumental or vocal parts are not doubled the variations from one performance to another, especially over time, may differ. Buddhist chant, for a contrasting example, is often performed in large groups where individual variations are weeded out (recall CD tracks 4 and 5).

The global circulation of the concept of the piece is worth contemplating in this context. What is the cultural value of a notated piece (as opposed to one orally transmitted)? Whose interest might such a notion serve? How does this link with notions of copyright and ownership—other value systems that circulate through the global economy? The use of notation has become increasingly important in the past few decades as traditional lifestyles give way to the five-day workweek, a capitalist economy, and a faster pace of life. Students now take lessons scheduled for an hour or two a week and might pay cash for them rather than cook or clean as in a pre-modern context. These changes brought on by new modes of transmission are more prominent in the urban centers than in rural areas and more prevalent in Thailand and Vietnam than in Burma/Myanmar, Cambodia, and Laos.

Thai and Burmese Notation.   Efforts to transcribe and adopt staff notation into Thai and Burmese music cultures found interesting parallels in the work of Phra Chen Duriyanga (recall the discussion of the Thai national anthem) and U Khin Zaw respectively. Both were publishing their transcriptions of Thai and Burmese traditional music in the 1940s and 50s, motivated by a need to preserve and codify their dying traditions. Both were trained in the Western tradition (in England) and had absorbed certain Western values regarding notation, permanence, preservation, and (perhaps to a lesser degree) standardization, and they also used Western theoretical models to "explain" their traditions. Phra Chen and U Khin Zaw were both connected to government ministries and nationalism movements that provided the backing to pursue their projects and a platform to disseminate their findings. The writings of each were widely distributed and at the time were regarded internationally as representative portraits of Thai and Burmese music. And yet, neither is quite representative of Burmese or Thai music from the perspective of the local professional musician.

Before World War II, U Khin Zaw, the head librarian at the University of Rangoon and an amateur musician, played oboe in the now obsolete Rangoon Philharmonic. In the late 1930s U Khin Zaw began to collect and transcribe many of Burma's classical songs (*thachin gyi*—great songs). In his capacity as librarian U Khin Zaw went to great lengths to preserve many transcribed songs and recordings from the first half of the century (predominantly those recorded on Columbia records) by creating an archives. Unfortunately, most all of these recordings, along with much of the library, were destroyed during the war. My teacher in Burma has exclaimed great appreciation for the song collections that U Khin Zaw made and the attention his work garnered for Burmese music, but little appreciation for his actual notations and theoretical writings, claiming that while he was Western trained, he was not trained in the Burmese tradition and, therefore, ill-equipped to deal with Burmese music.

Similarly, in reference to reproductions of Phra Chen Duriyanga notations American scholar Terry Miller writes "[T]here is no doubt that he was European in training and lacked traditional Thai training. Indeed, he was thought of as a Western musician in Thailand. Some Thai musicians also assert that he was at least partly European in lineage as well. The booklet includes most conventional wisdom regarding Thai music, but sheds little or no light on the matter from a Thai perspective" (Miller 1983). While Western training familiarized Khin Zaw and Duriyanga with staff notation, their lack of training in Burmese and Thai music respectively makes their notations suspect.

Indigenous notation systems other than Western staff notation exist in Burma/Myanmar, Thailand and Vietnam but are only used as memory aides and would never be seen in a professional performance context. Even today in the state schools of arts in Myanmar, Thailand, Cambodia and Vietnam, rote memorization of repertoire is still predominant. Indigenous notations in both Thailand and Burma started to become common in the 1930s and 40s. Luang Pradit Phairao (historically fictionalized in the film *The Overture*) is credited with being the first to create a specifically Thai notation system (Myers Moro 1993: 142). In Thailand, notation has become increasingly common for the music of the two-string bowed lutes (*saw duang* and *saw u*) and the zithers (*jakhe* and *khim*) as can be seen in Figure 5.3. While five-line staff notation is occasionally used, more common are generic versions of pieces written out in tablature (specific to an instrument or instrument type) or pitch notation (either written in Thai solfège or numbers).

Burmese musicians similarly adopted a local form of written cipher notation where written numbers indexed the pitches to be played. This notation system is still frequently used today and can be found in instructional books for *pattala*, *saung*, and *patt waing* (Figures 2.2, 2.7, 2.8, CD track 6, 9 and 10) and is often used by students to jot down melodies. Of the instructional books directed at the general public, most use the type of tablature shown in Figure 5.3 and very few, until the late 1990s, use Western notation.

FIGURE 5.3 *Thai notation for saw duang (Myers-Moro 1993: 149). Two lines of notation. One for each of the two Sau Duang strings. Numbers represent finger positions, not pitch. This contemporary notation uses Arabic numerals (rather than Thai) for fingerings.*

Burmese cipher notation provides the two parts and the lyrics (Figure 5.4). Occasionally the notation is written with each of the two parts, as below (recall the discussion of the two-part basis of Burmese music in Chapter 2), and often only the primary upper part is notated. Accomplished musicians generally only require one part and would infer the secondary lower accompanying part. The notation is flexible enough to guide playing on any instrument yet each would, of course, present its own version of the melody. Bar lines are drawn after every cycle of the implied *si* and *wa* (bell and clapper) pattern, in this case *wa let si* (see Chapter 2).

Unique to this notation is the numbering system that reflects the downward motion of most Burmese melodies. In a Burmese seven-note scale, downward motion is considered natural. If you ask a Burmese musician to play a scale they will begin at the upper tonic, descend down an octave and return in ascending pitches up to the top. Thus, the scale descends with the prescribed numbers 1 to 7 (1 2 3 4 5 6 7 1 or ၁ ၂ ၃ ၄ ၅ ၆ ၇ ၁). This contrasts with Western cipher notation that would depict the same passage as (1 7 6 5 4 3 2 1). The note names for the seventh, sixth, etc., descending scale pitches are drawn from the fingerings on the *hne* (Figure 2.3). The scale is laid out in descending order as successive fingers are placed on the bored holes of the *hne*, i.e. down the tube

FIGURE 5.4 *Burmese cipher notation (notated by U Han Sein) for the beginning piece* Tan Tya Teh Shin *as heard on CD track 25. The top line is the vocal text and the bottom two lines are for each hand of the pattala. Burmese numbers from 1–7 are* ၁ ၂ ၃ ၄ ၅ ၆ ၇.

away from the face, thus descending in pitch (or fingers) while ascending in number.

ACTIVITY 5.6 *Transnotate the above cipher notation into Arabic numbers. Listen again to CD track 25 and write in X and O notations for si and wa respectively. Try now to sing this melody on your own or play it on any instrument of your choice.*

Cipher notation that uses Burmese numerals, and descending numbers, is slowly falling out of fashion as more and more Arabic numbers (1, 2, 3) are used. When Burmese musicians use Arabic numbers they conform to a global status quo, as it were, and use ascending numbers. Older notations that use Burmese numerals retain the descending scale pitch naming, while newer notation that uses Arabic numerals adopts the rising scale pitch numbering. Thus, if your first note is C, the 2nd note in Burmese notation would be B, in Arabic notation it would be D. Cipher notations like that shown in Figure 5.4 would rarely be used in a performance context. These systems are almost exclusively used for pedagogical and retention purposes. Occasionally, they are used in a recording studio as a composer is working with the studio musicians. In the 21st century, particularly in the urban areas, if notation is used during a rehearsal it is most always an Arabic-numbered, cipher notation.

During the 20th century many of the governments in mainland Southeast Asia have sponsored preservation projects that would notate a portion of the traditional (usually court-related) music in Western staff notation. In Burma/Myanmar the irony of translating this tradition into Western staff notation is compounded by the fact that very few professional musicians know how to read it. Of those that do, none use it in their day-to-day musical performances or rehearsals, and might only as a means of picking out a Western melody from an international book. Staff notation (like that transcribed in Figure 5.5) is almost never used, in fact, I have only met two or three Burmese musicians who use staff notation to play Burmese music (see below), and in those cases the notation was employed to preserve an already memorized piece.

While publication and distribution of staff-notated songs may communicate uniqueness and valorize a tradition, it also presents certain problems to the tradition. The very act of notation, putting to paper a diverse oral tradition, standardizes the music. Determining one

FIGURE 5.5   Tan Tya Teh Shin *in staff notation for pattala.*

definitive version of a song potentially kills the diversity of an oral tradition. My observations reveal significant tensions between the forces of standardization (embodied in notation projects that seek to standardize or seek to impose specific uses of the notation) and oral keepers of the tradition. The preface to one early (1964) notation project reads:

> The aim and object of the Ministry of Union Culture is to explore every possible avenue for the preservation of archaic or traditional Burmese Songs in their original essence both in tune and style.
> …With a *view to translate it into reality* this book containing thirteen classical songs…is published for the first time of its kind.

A "view to translate…(the tradition) into reality." Now in print, the tradition becomes real. Turning the tradition into tangible controllable objects and events such as sheet music (as well as performing arts competitions and universities) legitimizes the tradition, and those that patronize it, for use in modern nation-state identity and unity politics. While many nations codified and catalogued their national traditions shortly after independence (and created national schools, competitions, museums, and libraries to house them), in Burma/Myanmar many of these standardizations have been created in the past fifteen years (see Douglas 2001) as a result of the changed cultural policies after the 1988 uprising. Globalization makes manifest a growing tension between the forces of standardization (embodied in notation projects and national schools) and oral traditions. Many of the people who seem to place high value in notation are, ironically, not musicians. It should be emphasized that simply because a notation exists does not mean that it will be used by musicians. What purpose, then, would these notations serve to a non-musician?

Pamela Moro frequently suggested to her informants in Thailand that the idea of notation derived from contact with the West. This idea was not wholeheartedly agreed upon (Myers-Moro 1993: 146). I found similar views in Burma/Myanmar, where an aggressive anti-colonial campaign was daily put forth by all the state controlled media. Several times throughout my research, I inadvertently referred to five-line staff notation as "Western notation." I was quickly corrected. Western culture—particularly British and American—is strongly denigrated in the state press. Elements of Western culture recognized as valuable, such as staff notation, are renamed *international* or even *universal*. As the five-line staff notation system becomes increasingly used throughout the country, its "Western" roots are masked.

The point of this is that, for most musicians and most of my teachers, competence in reading Western notation—or, rather, "International Notation"—was irrelevant to their activities playing Burmese music; such notation seemed to be exclusively reserved for reading Western music. The violinist, U Tin Yi, having spent his career as a studio musician (see Douglas 2005), is spending his retirement with Western classical music, playing Vivaldi concertos and Bach suites. He enthusiastically reads all Western sheet music that he is able to acquire. When asked to play Burmese music he will either study the *Maha Gita* (great song) texts to recollect pieces or, in some cases, consult the cipher notation that he, as a student, learned from his teacher. In several cases he had actually notated Burmese melodies into Western notation, yet these were never used to recollect or learn new pieces. While I was in recording studios and the studio musicians were learning pieces to accompany a singer, Western staff notation was not used, even by those familiar with how to use it. Instead, a copy of the lyric sheet would offer enough clues to the melodic contour and the "basic tune" for musicians to then insert their own parts. (see Figure 5.6)

As with all generalizations about human behavior, some exceptions are notable. Using "international notation," my lessons with the *saung* master U Myint Maung were unique. He adopted staff notation to try and make his teaching more effective. Over the past thirty years U Myint Maung has transcribed in Western staff notation more than 200 of the *thachin kyi* songs (refer back to Chapter 2). Prior to his death in 2001, U Myint Maung used staff notation of his own transcriptions with most of his students, as he felt it important for them to learn how to read music. While learning various pieces on the *saung* (Figure 2.5, CD track 9) I used his transcriptions, yet I was instructed by U Myint Maung to memorize the piece as quickly as possible. Only after memorizing the piece, and thus no longer using the notation, was I making music. Then I could start interpreting the piece and adding my own variations. The notation

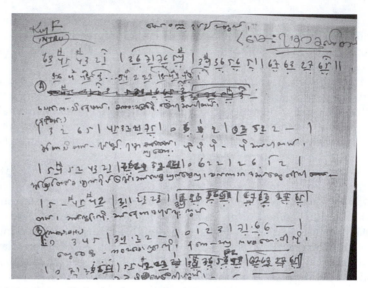

FIGURE 5.6 *Skeletal cipher notation for a composition by U Ko Ko (Gita Lulin Maung Ko Ko) for use in a studio recording session. Note the hybrid qualities of the notation—"Key F" which only refers to the tonic and "Intro" are in English. Cipher notation is written in Arabic numerals (not Burmese) and lyrics are written with Burmese script. Current notational practice in the country is very much a fusion of Western and Burmese elements.*

here operates as an expedient way to learn a piece (less time intensive on the teacher as a student can be sent home with the notation) and as a memory aid.

In the past five years as more and more people have become educated in Western notation, a few authors have notated and published their version of select classical pieces. Relatively inexpensive notation software programs have allowed individual authors (independent of institutional patronage) to notate and publish. Ko Shoon Myaing, son of one of Burma/Myanmar's most famous composers Myoma Nyein, compiled in 2001 the volume *International Notation and Myanmar Classical Songs*. It is one of the more prominent of these publications. Written in both English and Burmese to an indistinct audience, the volume is very much a reflection of Burma/Myanmar's ever increasing global relations—despite its isolation. On the one hand the volume appeals to Burmese nationals to recognize their classical traditions via an internationally recognized platform; on the other it is quite accessible to and marketed to foreigners in the country's tourist shops. It contains brief biographies of composers and an essay on the development of music from Gregorian chant through to Burmese music—a lineage that is obviously quite forced. From his forward;

> ...it is the historical duty of every country and its people to preserve its national heritage, its true music which is the sound basis for national culture. Likewise, it is our duty to relay to the younger generation to make them see the need to be abreast of the times: the new modern music and the universal use of staff-notation system.
>
> As the writer is a Myanmar national, I embrace the concept that "Myanmar Classical Music" is the bedrock of Myanmar music, and I hope and urge that every Myanmar would accept my concept. Thus, the essence of this short thesis is to reveal the authentic heritage of our past teachers and to correctly preserve our heritage with the universal staff-notation system. (Ko Shoon Myaing 2001)

Overt nationalist appeals speak not only to the climate of music standardization and notation projects in Burma/Myanmar but also to the quest for legitimacy that (some) authors feel can only be gained through adoption and use of global systems of transmission and distribution. Classicization, thus, is often an overtly nationalist project.

GLOBAL INSTRUMENTS AND MASS MEDIA

The introduction of different musical instruments to the region and the distribution of sounds and images through the mass media provide further evidence of the ongoing process of globalization. The royal musicians of King Mindon's Mandalay court (1860s-70s) took to the piano on the king's request after it was presented as a gift from an Italian ambassador. Early approaches to this exotic instrument naturally were informed by Burmese concepts of music. The white keys of the piano became equivalent to the keys of the *pattala* (CD track 10 or the drums of the *patt waing*, CD track 6 and 7). Musicians experimented with tunings to approximate their own scale. This consisted of raising the fourth and lowering the seventh scale degrees necessary to modulate between different Burmese modes (pg. 45–6). The practice of re-tuning the piano generated many disputes in the early part of the century. In facilities that were shared by both Burmese and British patrons such as movie houses where live music accompanied film, the piano would have to be tuned in even-tempered tuning for English movies and back to Burmese tuning for Burmese films. The combination of radical tuning adjustments (as many as several times a week) and the hot humid tropical climate were very rough on pianos. Piano makers, setting up shops in Rangoon, shortly thereafter adjusted with extra-fortified pianos designed for the tropical climate (Wright 1910).

The increased facility of ten fingers (over two mallets for the *pattala* or two hands for the *patt waing*) led to significant increase in virtuosity and musical complexity. Eventually the black notes of the piano were incorporated into pieces in secondary (passing, non-functional or ornamental) positions. Today Myanmar has a multitude of excellent virtuosic pianists. Gita Lulin Maung Ko Ko (or U Ko Ko) (1930–2007) was one of the country's most prominent pianist/composers over the past fifty years (Figure 5.7). CD track 26 offers his piano version of

FIGURE 5.7   *Pianist composer Gita Lulin Maung Ko Ko in 2005.*

the same *yodaya* piece that he played on the *pattala* (CD track 10). It is quite common for Burmese musicians to excel on several instruments: all *patt waing* players will play *pattala* and many will also play the piano.

> ACTIVITY 5.7 *Listen to the two different versions of the Yodaya piece "Myaman Giri" on pattala (CD track 10) and piano (CD track 26). Composed in the 18th century by Myawadi U Sa based on Thai melodies that he learned from prisoners of war, it is a well-known piece in Burma/Myanmar today.*
>
> *After listening to each version several times attempt to sing along with the melody. Notice how the contour of the melody remains while the elaborations found on each instrument are unique.*
>
> *Now listen more closely. Myaman Giri has two contrasting sections (A and B). On the* pattala *U Ko Ko presents a version with an AAB form, while on the piano he plays AABB. With a clock try and identify when each section begins.*
>
> *Listen now to U Aung Shein play a version of the same piece on Burmese style slide guitar (CD track 27). What additional variations can you identify? As this version was recorded for my own lessons it is, understandably, the most unornamented of the versions.*

Primarily through the rise of the Burmese film industry in the 1930s and 1940s musicians added a wider and wider variety of sounds to their pallet. Film, as in India, was the central medium for distribution of popular songs, as most films were musicals. The film sold the songs and the songs sold the film—the two industries were intimately intertwined. The addition of new instruments for use in this media expanded to include violin (*tayaw*) and piano (*sandaya*) as well as saxophone, trombone, trumpet, slide guitar, and banjo in addition to traditional instruments (*saung, pattala* and *saing waing*).

Though the colonials and the economic elite considered film, compared to the theater tradition, low art, the opportunities for financial and popular success were much greater. As with traditional theater (as well as models for films coming from India), many of these early films were musicals. Silent films, popular in Burma into the 1940s (much later than in other countries), provided small orchestras, guitarists, and single pianists with opportunities for composition and accompaniment in a fast-growing popular medium. Film was the primary medium by which the sound of foreign instruments was introduced to Burma. By the 1950s, film was much more popular than traditional theater and the success of the Burmese film industry peaked in this decade, with well over one hundred pictures per year coming out of Rangoon alone. By contrast the first decade of the 21st century finds fewer than ten films produced each year as low-budget video production backed by prerecorded music replaces film.

In order, of course, for the piano and later the violin, mandolin, and guitar to be usefully adapted into a Burmese context (for film and other uses), several stylistic and practical hurdles had to be reconciled: namely the tuning system and harmonic organization. Through the 1940s, as mentioned above, pianos were occasionally retuned to the traditional Burmese scale, with sharp 4 and flat 7 scale degrees, and pitch flexible instruments like the slide guitar and violin became more and more prominent. With the introduction in the 1920s and 1930s of imported fixed-pitch instruments such as the saxophone, clarinet, and trumpet, this practice of readjusting to traditional tuning gradually disappeared. Recent pitch-flexible electronic keyboards have allowed players to experiment with and revive earlier tuning systems. U Ko Ko before his death in 2007 was a leading advocate for a return to un-tempered, Burmese style, tuning. Such "experiments" cannot be used with Western tuned or tempered instruments.

Early 20th century approaches to Western instruments disregarded the chromatic possibilities of the piano's black notes and included a two-part style that mimicked traditional techniques: the two-mallet or two-hand technique of the *pattala* (xylophone) and *patt waing* (drum circle) and the two-finger technique of the *saung gauk* (arched harp, Figure 2.7, CD track 9). This two-part style, with its roots in Burmese court music, can also be found in the approaches to guitar and mandolin playing that took hold in the earlier part of the century.

The guitar starts to appear in early Burmese recordings and in the accompaniment of silent films as early as the 1920s. The adoption of the guitar at this time appears extensively in art music and popular music. The early guitars adapted were lap style Hawaiian slide guitars on which could be produced sliding technique that imitates vocal interpretations of text (CD track 27). Several octogenarian guitarists with whom I spoke talked favorably of the Kalamazoo guitar—a Hawaiian style guitar with a metal support (truss) rod in the neck and a plywood top which made them strong and cheap.

The Kalamazoo guitar can be traced back to the Gibson factory in Kalamazoo, Michigan that manufactured them between 1930 and 1960. Early approaches to Burmese guitar started with adaptation of the *thachin gyi* (great song) court repertoire. This is demonstrated on CD track 27 with another version of "Myaman Giri" played by guitarist U Aung Shein.

From Activity 5.7 you will be sufficiently familiar with the song "Myaman Giri" to listen for other details of Burmese instrumental technique: the use of a teeter-totter (*maung-hnin*) technique used on many traditional instruments (*patt waing, pattala, saung*). *Maung-hnin* is a musical technique that alternates octaves and creates a multitude of 9–8 suspensions combined with supporting tones a fourth or fifth below.

ACTIVITY 5.8 *Listen to CD track 27 and identify the maung hnin technique most clearly heard at 0:04–07 seconds, 0:23–27 seconds, 0:53–55 seconds. Can you identify more subtle manifestation of this technique? Listen again to CD track 9. The saung gauk is played with a similar right hand (first finger and thumb) technique. If you can identify any maung hnin (alternating finger and thumb) passages, take note of the timing in the recording.*

Tuning of the guitar for this piece is CGFCGF. Such tuning allows for accessible octaves and with the slide, one does not have to conform to Western tuning and can more clearly imitate Burmese style singing. This type of tuning also avoids the major and minor third and the Western harmonic implications of those two notes. The two-part style adapted to Western instruments is a distinctive feature of early Burmese popular music and can be found on many of the first recordings made of Burmese music.

As early as 1903, the Gramophone Company of India had made recordings of local artists in Southeast Asia. By 1910, over 500 Burmese recordings had been pressed (Gronow 1981, 258). These recording sessions were drawn from short trips from India on rushed schedules, after which master recordings were taken back to Calcutta for mass pressing. Recordings were then returned to Burma for sale on the local market. Export, processing, and resale of raw materials was a major money-making part of the British Empire. Columbia Records, His Master's Voice (HMV, known in Burma as the "Dog Brand"), and the A-1 Film and Recording Company were the largest companies working in pre-WWII Burma. These companies catered to two different, yet overlapping, markets. Columbia and HMV recorded many of the more traditional classical/court-related styles, including much of the theatrical *pwe* (discussed in Chapter 2) repertoire, and A-1 recorded a more modernized international style.

In 1960, when the film *Never on Sunday* won an Oscar for its title song written by Manos Hadjidakis, it quickly was adopted in Burma and used in Burmese films and theater. U Tin and U Maung Maung now in their 70s and 80s respectively (Figure 5.8) remember well playing this song for Burmese films during the 1960s. Their immediate adoption of this song into a Burmese context speaks to the cosmopolitan nature of these musical styles and these musicians. CD track 28 offers an example of the song adapted into a Burmese context and shows the adoption of another global instrument, the banjo. This song, found in Burmese movies, was understood by many Burmese audiences as a Burmese song.

FIGURE 5.8   *U Tin (guitar) and U Maung Maung (banjo) videotaped by the author.*

The Vietnamese implementation of the guitar provides an interesting parallel and contrast to the guitar in Burma/Myanmar. As has been mentioned, Chinese musical influence on Vietnamese music has been significant, with many of the country's instruments more closely related to Chinese instruments (zithers, two stringed bowed lutes) than with those of their Southeast Asian neighbors.

In Chapter 2 I discussed the prominence of *đàn* stringed instruments (*đàn bầu, đàn tranh, đàn nhi*). With high frets and loose strings, these instruments offer musicians the opportunity to manipulate particular pitches. Specific ornaments or vibrato on certain tones is necessary in order to conform to the modal system found in Vietnamese music. String vibrations, slides, and bends reflect vocal idiosyncracies and point to the close connection between melody and linguistic intonation. How then would Vietnamese musicians approach the guitar (inevitably) introduced to the region in the later part of the 19th and early part of the 20th century?

Musicians found venues for experimenting with Vietnamese guitar (*đàn ghi-ta* or *lục huyền cầm*) styles in urban contemporary music contexts such as *cải lương* theater (CD track 16). As in Burma, the guitar was an important global instrument to adopt for cosmopolitan or global popular contexts and was easily used in progressive film and theater music. Also like in Burma, the instrument was adapted in specific ways to fit into local understandings and aesthetics. While in Burma this meant different tunings and the incorporation of a slide, in Vietnam loose strings and a carved (scalloped) fret board allow performers to bend and manipulate notes akin to the manipulation of notes heard on the *đàn tranh* or the *đàn bầu*.

Kim Sinh, born in 1930, is a master of the Vietnamese style guitar and can be heard on CD track 29. Blind since shortly after his birth, he taught himself to play the *đàn nguyet* (lute) and eventually adopted the *đàn nguyet* technique to the modified guitar. He played in French dance halls during the colonial period and is known for his guitar versions of *cải lương* songs. "Li Giao Duyen" (CD track 29) is Kim Sinh's arrangement of a southern Vietnamese *cải lương* song on which can be heard distinctly Vietnamese slides, bends, and ornaments comparable to the approaches taken to string instruments on CD tracks 14, 15, and 16.

Changing Contexts. Throughout the 1930s, 1940s, and early 1950s the communities in major commercial ports developed a growing interest in Western big band jazz. Recall the interest in jazz on the part of the present king of Thailand (pg. 103). Nightclubs were established, catering to these musical interests and touring musicians (many from the Philippines) performed at the more popular venues in all of the major cities. Visits from jazz greats such as Count Basie (Figure 5.9), Duke Ellington, and Benny Goodman reinforced an interest in big band jazz in ballroom dancing and in the American Tin Pan Alley music repertorie.

While not entirely even in its distribution throughout the region, radio, television, and the Internet have radically changed the production and distribution networks. In the past few decades, music making throughout the world has changed through the increased affordability of home computer recording programs and relatively inexpensive publishing (print and audio) opportunities. In many Southeast Asian countries the ability to maintain copyright control cannot keep up with the changing technologies. In Burma and Cambodia, to a greater degree than in their neighboring countries, most income from a recording comes from the

FIGURE 5.9   *Count Basie with Burmese musician U Hla Htut.*

reproduction of the physical medium rather than through royalty collection by a performing rights organization. For example, no copyright money would be collected through the sale of the popular song lyric (and guitar chord) booklets seen in Figure 5.10 or from duplicated cassettes, or CDs. Income is generated through copies rather than through royalties. Artists themselves, therefore, often are directly involved in various tape/CD duplication endeavors.

Technological advances have contributed to an ever-increasing pace of change. Given the political struggles and uneven distribution of resources throughout the region, technological changes have not been evenly felt across the Southeast Asian peninsula. Affluent youth in Bangkok and more recently in Vietnam have led the region in adaptation and creative distribution of musics. Throughout all of the urban centers in Southeast Asia today mass media is quite accessible. Piracy of audio and video recordings is rampant with easy access to every new musical development from the Western world as well as India, China, and Japan. Pirating of recordings onto cheap cassette tapes in the 1980s

FIGURE 5.10 *Song lyric booklets for popular cassettes on the street in downtown Yangon/Rangoon, a complementary distribution medium. Lyric booklets that often include guitar chords reflect a culture of informal music production in the homes of music fans.*

and 1990s and onto CDs and VCD ('Video Compact Disc' a cheaper and lower quality medium than DVD) today quickly spreads musical ideas, sounds, and images. The state control over television images has moderated this to some degree yet black market products are readily available for those that wish them.

Internet access for urban Southeast Asia has, like much of the world, radically changed the way that musicians (especially contemporary popular musicians) have produced, recorded, and marketed themselves. Websites and MySpace accounts for many artists and genres have become a central and cost-effective way to perform and advertise.

ACTIVITY 5.9   *Choose one of the countries from mainland Southeast Asia.*

Search for popular musics distributed on the Internet (YouTube, MySpace, etc).

Try and find the top three artists from the country you have · chosen (of course such a list will be constantly changing and contested).

What makes them identifiably Burmese, Thai, Cambodian, or Vietnamese? Are there features of the sound, dress, or image that are recognizably local?

What features of the music would you associate with global traditions? Share your discoveries with your classmates.

IMMIGRATION AND DIASPORA

The varieties of music that get produced as Southeast Asian communities move abroad—providing different contexts for old sounds, new instruments, and styles with which to create novel compositions, and new production and distribution opportunities—is truly staggering. Ethnomusicological studies of immigrant and diasporic communities also provide insight into the retention, adaptation, and/or rejection of particular cultural identities, as individuals struggle to define themselves and their communities in a new environment. Immigration of peoples from mainland Southeast Asia to the United States and Canada has taken a wide variety of forms from voluntary to forced: moving for opportunity or fleeing from terror.

Case Studies in Cambodian American Music. Through three brief cases of new Khmer music in the United States I will highlight some of the exciting musical movements in Cambodian American music. Each musical example points to the strength of Cambodian identity, the reclaiming of that identity after the genocide of the 1970s, and the inter-relatedness of cultural identity with the flow of global ideas, images, and styles.

praCH. Though born in Cambodia, Prach Ly was raised in Long Beach, California, home to the largest Khmer community outside of Cambodia. Amid the resurgence of Khmer classical and folk traditions in both the U.S. and Cambodia, praCH combines samples of traditional Khmer music (folk and *pinn peat*) and Khmer Rouge propaganda speeches with hip-hop styles (CD track 30). Considered Cambodia's first rap star even though he resides outside of the country, praCH raps a memoir of the Cambodian experience in both Khmer and English, relaying horror stories of life under Pol Pot, as relayed to him from family members who survived. He made his first demo tape in 2000, a low budget compilation created in his parent's garage and copied for members of the Long Beach Khmer community. *Dalama: The End'n' Is Just the Beginnin'* made no noticeable impact in the United States. However, unbeknown to him, a pirated copy found its way to Cambodia distributed under the title Khmer rouge rap. It quickly became the number one album in the country (see Schlund-Vials 2008) and launched a new genre of pop music. At that time praCH had not been back to Cambodia since he left as a toddler. His song "Resurrec" (CD track 30, for lyrics see Figure 5.11) speaks to Cambodian history and to life in America.

Through songs like "Resurrec" (CD track 30) the Cambodian genocide is remembered and its many stories preserved, while at the same time the community is compelled to move forward and beyond. praCh re-articulates a Cambodian American identity and through the acceptance of the song in Cambodia it also plays a role in the construction of contemporary Khmer identity. He speaks to the past while rooted in the present through his mixing of *pinn peat* (elsewhere on the album) with electronic bass, mixing English and Khmer languages, and reviving historical texts (Khmer Rouge speeches) under contemporary presentation. In so doing, and through reference to other humanitarian atrocities, praCh's work links to other Cambodian American cultural

I love my land to death,
a child of the Killing Fields.
NorthstarResurrec,
Generation X what's next?
It's time for us to heal.
We've been suffering for decades,
decades of genocide.
Annihilation of generations,
a "demon-stration" on Khmer.
Now why do we do what we do?
like Hitlers to the Jews,
Whites to the Blacks,
they act like we (are) slaves.
I rather be back where I was born,
than here confused and dazed
I love America... but anyways.

FIGURE: 5.11   *Excerpt of lyrics to "Resurrec," from Dalama: The End'n' Is Just the Beginnin', 2000.*

producers "who transnationally re-imagine Cambodian nationhood and selfhood" (Schlund-Vials 2008).

ACTIVITY 5.10   *Listen multiple times praCH's "Resurrec". Find a complete set of the lyrics online. Do you think a hip-hop style is appropriate for relaying his message? Why or Why not?*

Dengue Fever. Dengue Fever is a six-member rock band from Los Angeles that was formed in 2001. Inspired by the 1960s-1970s psychedelic rock music scene in Cambodia (pre Khmer Rouge), Dengue Fever reinterprets many of those songs and writes original material inspired by Cambodian pop icons like Rous Sareysothea and Sin Sisamouth. American musicians Ethan and Zac Holtzman joined up with female Cambodian singer Chhom Nimol, a well-known karaoke singer from Cambodia. Nimol had moved to America and was working in a nightclub in the "Little Phnom Penh" area of Long Beach, California. Zac Holtzman, inspired by a trip to Cambodia, was looking for a Khmer

singer to front the band. With five male performers fronted by the female Khmer-singing Chhom Nimol, decked out in self-designed glit-
tery night-club dresses, the band visually as well as sonically performs
a dialogue between two seemingly disparate cultures.

After three highly acclaimed albums (readily available online and
with many band videos on YouTube) the band toured Cambodia in 2007
with a crew to film the documentary *Sleepwalking Through the Mekong*
(see www.sleepwalkingthroughthemekong.com). While Chhom Nimol
reunites with her home community and fans, her bandmates seek out
traditional musicians and other local musical inspirations. The film
reveals much of what is both enjoyable and confusing about global processes and cultural exchanges, as the music that results cannot easily be
localized as Californian or Cambodian—their music is a hybrid of each
enjoyed by fans in both countries.

Where Elephants Weep. Commissioned by the Cambodian Living
Arts project (see pg. 117), *Where Elephants Weep* is a Cambodian-American
opera that had its American premier in 2008. The composer, Him Sophy,
who lost two brothers to the Khmer Rouge, draws from a wide range of
musical sources as he mixes Khmer traditional court music with modern Cambodian and Western rock, pop and rap, Cambodian lullabies,
and Khmer Rouge propaganda songs performed with a rock band, a
pinn peat ensemble, a string quartet, synthesizers, and other Khmer folk
instruments. See <http://www.whereelephantsweep.net>

The opera, like the two musical examples above, visits the themes
of trauma recovery and a return to the homeland. Also similar to the
cultural productions of praCH and Dengue Fever is the role the opera
plays in the re-articulation and re-clamation of cultural identity. In
Where Elephants Weep, Sam, a refugee from the Khmer Rouge genocide,
leaves America and returns to Cambodia. Searching for his roots in his
native culture, he falls in love with Bopha, a Cambodian pop-star who
was born on the very day that the Khmer Rouge invaded Phnom Penh.
Torn between two worlds Sam and Bopha, an intercontinental Romeo
and Juliet singing in both Khmer and English, struggle to reconcile tradition with modernity. How is one to be both Khmer and part of the
global community?

The transnational or globalized character of all three of these projects is central to their success and essential to the reconstruction of a
post-genocidal Khmer identity. Natural to each of these projects is the
mixing of traditional instruments and sounds with international ones
as well as singing in both English and Khmer, often in the same song.

Each also works to cultivate an audience in both the United States and in Cambodia.

ACTIVITY 5.11   *Visit the websites for each of these projects.*

www.mujestic.com
www.sleepwalkingthroughthemekong.com
www.whereelephantsweep.net

Listen to and watch the samples provided. Write a short essay that addresses these questions. In what ways are these projects similar? In what ways are they different? In what ways are they informed by globalization? In what different ways do they each deal with conflict, recovery and modernization?

REVOLUTION ON THE INTERNET

During the Saffron Revolution of Sept 2007 (see pg. 119) digital technology played a significant role in not simply transmitting information out of the country but in organizing and coordinating activities within. Such reflexive behavior on the part of the participants was the single most significant difference between this and other political uprisings in the country. Those marching and those supporting the protesters documented the event with video, photography, and audio recordings of the event because they new the world would watch. Despite all the attempts by their own government to control the flow of information they knew that their lives were connected to people outside of the country.

Cameras, cell phones, and video all clicked away, documenting the images and circulating them on the Internet for the world to witness. The obvious result of this was a translocation of the conflict into the Burmese expatriate community and the global community at large. After several days of protest the Burmese military shut down the Internet throughout the entire country but images continued to flow internationally. Immediate response came from the international community with condemnation of the crackdown or at least calls for restraint, sympathy to the victims, calls for UN resolutions, further EU and US sanctions, and assertive statements by globally-recognized Buddhist figures like the Dalai Lama and Thich Nhat Hanh.

The images found on YouTube and other video sharing sites provides a somewhat different perspective on the conflict. Dozens of Saffron Revolution vignettes appeared online in the months following the event. These "homemade" videos consist of visual footage (video and still pictures) of the events on the street backed by a wide range of music, which (usually) was not Burmese. Of the many Saffron Revolution vignettes found on the Internet since the event I have not been able to find one that employs the sounds of the *Metta Sutta* (recall Chapter 4 pg. 121). The *Metta Sutta*, one of the most significant sounds of the protest on the street, symbolizes much of the non-violent character of the protest. Instead, other musical traditions with other political associations are superimposed upon the images. For many it seems, pictures of bloodied monks would make a more significant impact not backed by Burmese music, monks chanting loving kindness, or audio clips from the event but, rather, sounds that indexed other types of protest (or comfort). Aggressive heavy metal, hip-hop, and reggae for many outside of Burma would index political protest; acoustic guitar ballads or hymns would provide comfort.

One contribution to this online commentary on the revolution came from a UK-based conglomerate of hip-hop inspired Burmese who produce under the label Myanmar Future Generation (sometimes Future Burmese Generation). The video and song "Let Us Be United" (CD track 31) is an assertive rap sung in Burmese (despite its English title) that resonates with other hip-hop related resistance musics. Angry lyrics admonishing the Burmese generals for attacking the monks ("stepping on the sons of Buddha"), ignoring their people ("the people are starving"), and distorting the country's history, ("Bogyoke [General Aung San] did not train the military just to kill") are accompanied by many of the photographic stills that circulated in the days after the protest. Many of the photos are violent images, with injured monks, burned cars, and dead bodies distributed globally to elicit both sympathy and anger.

People are starving, religion is being destroyed,
people are being killed, they're lusting for power

If the armed forces are for the people, help them
But you cheated your benefactor.

You stepped your foot on the sons of Buddha, dared to kill innocent lives.
Bogyoke did not train the military just to kill, our cries not recorded in history.

Chorus: We are hungry; all prices are going up,
Sangha's *blood is being shed, people are being de-spirited.*

Numerous other videos created by Burmese expatriates and by non-Burmese about the Saffron Revolution include many of the same images. Some of the musics accompanying these other videos include: military marching songs; the Filipino resistance song "Oras Nas" associated with mass demonstrations in the Philippines; the Nu Metal band Korn's "Falling Away from Me" that contemplates suicide in the face of struggle; Led Zepplin's "Stairway to Heaven"; Simon and Garfunkel's "Sounds of Silence"; sacred harp hymns from Appalachia; and a huge array of generic ballad rock songs with which I am less familiar. Most of the selected soundtracks are not Burmese and have associations with other political movements. None of them were noticeably Buddhist.

Despite political and economic sanctions, technology has connected Myanmar to the world in novel ways. The Saffron Revolution should be examined within the context of Burma's decades long quest for political liberation but, despite its image as a hermit country and the xenophobic tendencies of its generals, it also is clearly part of global economic, political, and media flows.

CONCLUSION

While the flow of resources, ideas, and people across borders has had regular and changing influence on economic, political, and cultural systems throughout the region, there is little doubt that the pace of change over the last century, and most significantly the past decade, has been enormous. The very fact that you are reading this book speaks to an array of educational values that embrace aspects of globalism that have changed significantly over the past several decades. Our understanding of the region has been both distorted and clarified through media representations—films, plays, recordings, and YouTube videos. While on the one hand global economic, political, and media trends have contributed to marginalizing already peripheral communities, they have also provided a platform for the underrepresented to make their voices heard in novel and exciting ways. Almost every facet of music and music making has been impacted by globalization—transmission practices, preservation, concertizing, and protest. While governments still play a significant role in shaping music cultures, they often do so using globally shared methods like creating national universities, standardizing repertoires, and notating and preserving songs. At the same time, even the most restrictive of government policies cannot contain the flow (in and out) of ideas, images and sounds, and the uses to which they are put in forging new identities and new alliances with other parts of the world.

Glossary

∞

Aerophone Instrument whose primary sound-procudicng medium is vibrating air

Ahlu Offering (Burmese)

Ayuthaya/Ayudhya Thai kingdom from 1350 to 1767

Akha Tibeto-Burman speaking people living in Northern Thailand, Burma and China

Angkor Watt/Ankor Vat Center of Khmer kingdom, temple complex in Cambodia

Angkar The Khmer Rouge rulers

Anyein/anyeint Burmese theater of music, women vocalist and comedians

Apsara Khmer "heavenly maidens"–dancers from the heavens; female supernatural dancers

Basakk Khmer village theater genre of Chinese origin

Cải lương/cai luong/gai luong Genre of popular theater from southern Vietnam

Cipher notation System of musical notation where numbers denote particular pitches

Chap Pair of medium-size cymbals connected by a cord, thinner than ching (Thai)

Chapei/chapey/chapei dong veng Popular long necked lute of Cambodia. It may have two or four strings, but tuned to two notes; a four-string chapei will have two pairs of identically tuned strings.

Chauk lon batt Set of six (sometimes more) drums in the saing waing (Burmese) ensemble

Chhap Pair of medium-size cymbals connected by a cord, thinner than chhing (Khmer)

Chin ethnic group from northern Burma

Ching   Pair of cymbals connected by a cord (Thai)

Chhing   Pair of cymbals connected by a cord (Khmer)

Đại nhạc   Ritual court music of Vietnam

Dana   Ritual exchange (Buddhism)

Đàn bầu/dan bau/dan doc huyen   Vietnamese monochord

Đân ca   Vietnamese folk song

Đàn nhị/đan nhi/đan co   Vietnamese (two stringed fiddle)

Đan nguyet   Vietnamese long-necked, moon-shaped lute

Đàn trahn/đan trahn   Vietnamese 16, 17, or 21 stringed zither

Đàn tỳ-bà   Vietnamese pear-shaped lute

Dana   Ritual exchange of giving, often to the sangha in exchange for merit. The practice of cultivating generosity.

Deva Raja   God King

Điệu   Vietnamese system of modes

Dhamma/dharma   The teachings of the Buddha

Dhamma rajika   God king

Đổi mới   "Renovation"; the term given to the Vietnamese economic reforms of the late 1980s

Doùpá/douphat   Burmese small, double-headed barrel drum

Hát   General Vietnamese term for singing and acting

Hátbôi/Hat boi   Central Vietnamese theater

Hát chèo tào/Hat cheo   Vietnamese theatre. Hát chèo is a popular, satirical folk play of northern Vietnam that combines folk songs and dances with humorous sketches criticizing the people's rulers. Some scholars theorize that it is an indigenous folk art.

Heterogeneous sound   Combining instruments with different timbres

Heterophony   "Different voices"; musical texture of one melody performed almost simultaneously and somewhat differently by multiple musicians.

Hmong   Sino-Tibetan upland group living in Laos, Thailand, Vietnam, and China

Hne/hnè   Burmese conical aerophone with quadruple-double reed (sometimes triple-double reed)

Homogeneous sound   Combining instruments with similar timbres

Homrong   Thai ceremonial suite/overture in classical music

Isan/Issan   Northeast Thailand

Jakhe   Thai three stringed zither (originally in crocodile shape)

Jataka   Story of a past life of the Buddha

Karen   Ethnic group from eastern Burma and western Thailand

Kachin   Ethnic group from northern Burma/Myanmar

Kamma/Karma   The sum of all actions. The results and consequences of all behavior, felt in this life or the next.

Kantrum   Khmer style music from Eastern Thailand

Khaen/khene/kaen   Free-reed aerophone found in Laos and Thailand

Khawng   Single, bossed gongs of Thailand

Khit haung   Oldies style. Burmese genre music played on Western instruments with Burmese style. Popular in the 1920–1950s.

Khloy   Khmer end-blown duct flute of bamboo

Khlui   Thai bamboo or wood fipple flute

Khmer   Majority ethnic group in the Kingdom of Cambodia

Khmer Rouge   Communist political organization of Cambodia

Khon/Khone   Masked dance-drama based on the Ramayana

Khong wong yai   Thai lower pitched gong circle

Khong wong let   Thai higher pitched gong circle

Khru   Thai teacher

Khrüng sai   Thai court entertainment ensemble of strings and flute

Kinh   The lowland Vietnamese population (see Việt)

Kong mong   Khmer single, suspended bossed gong

Kong thom   Khmer high pitch gong circle

Kong tauch   Khmer lower pitch gong circle

Kong wong yai/Khawng wong yai   Thai gong circle of sixteen bossed gongs

Krapeu   Three-stringed floor zither of Cambodia

Krapp   Khmer pair of bamboo or wood clappers

Kruang sai   Thai string ensemble

Kyam   Mon three stringed crocodile-shaped zither. Similar to the thai jakhe. Mi kyaung in Burmese.

Kyi waing   Burmese gong circle

Lai   Melodic modes found in Laotian lam

Lam sing   Faster paced contemporary version of morlam

Lingwin   Burmese cymbals

Luk thung   "Children of the Fields." Thai musical tradition drawn from rural country areas. Often referred to as Thai country music.

Mon   Ethnic group of southern Burma and Thailand

Maha Gita   Literally "great songs." A collection of song texts passed down through the Burmese courts.

Mahayana Buddhism   "The Great Vehicle." The Northern branch of Buddhism found in China, Korea, Japan and Vietnam

Mahori/Mohori   Thai/Cambodian music ensemble comprised of xylophones, gong circles, and bowed fiddle (no pi/sralai aerophone)

Maung   Burmese gong

Maung Hnin   "Teeter totter" alternating octave technique in Burmese music

Morlam/Mawlum/Molam   Poetic singing style found in Issan, Thailand, and Laos. Accompanied by khaen.

Meru   A mythical mountain at the center of the physical, metaphysical and spiritual universe. Many wats and pagodas are symbolic representations of the idea.

Nat   Animistic spirit found in Burma/Myanmar

Nat Kadaw   Wife of the nat spirit. Spirit medium for communicating with the nat spirits.

Nat Pwe   Festival or ceremony for nat propitiation and possession

Ozi   A tall goblet shaped drum found in multiple forms in upper Burma/Myanmar

Pagoda   A shrine containing a real or symbolic relic of the Buddha (see stupa)

Parrita   Buddhist chants for offering or portection

Pasabou   One of the melodic modes utilized by the Burmese saing waing ensemble

Pattala   Burmese 21 keyed bamboo xylophone

Pattam   Monastic refusal of donataions

Patt Sa   Drum food. Tuning paste for tuning the drums of the Burmese Patt Waing.

Patt Ma   Large drum found in saing waing ensemble

Patt Waing   Burmese drum circle of 21 tuned drums

Pali   Indo-Aryan language; the language of the earliest extant Buddhist scriptures

Paya pwe   Pagoda festival

Phi   Animistic spirits in Thailand

Phin   Issan/Laotian plucked lute

Pin Pia   Thai monochord

Pi-nai   Reed aerophone instrument in Thai piphat ensemble

Piphat   Thai court/ritual ensemble of aerophones, idiophones, and membranophones used to accompany ritual and theatre

Piphat mon   Piphat ensemble used by the Mon ethnicity in Southern Burma and Thailand

Pinn peat   Court ensemble of Cambodia. Used for theater and dance accompaniment

Pwe   Burmese play, celebration, ritual, or event

Qeej/gaeng   Hmong free-reed aerophone

Ramakien   Thai version of the Ramayana story

Ramayana   Hindu epic story of the god Rama

Rammana   Thai shallow wooden drum with calfskin membrane

Ranat ek   Thai wooden xylophone (high pitched)

Ranat thum   Thai wooden xylophone (lower pitched)

Reamker   Khmer verision of the Ramayana

Robaim   Khmer pure dance from the Royal Court (as opposed to dance drama)

Roeung   Khmer narrative dance or dance drama from the Royal court

Rubato   Ebb and flow in the pace of the basic beat

Sangha   The order of monks in Buddhism

Saing waing/hsaiñwaiñ/hsaing waing Burmese classical music and theater ensemble

Saung-gauk/Saung 16 stringed arched harp of Burma

Saw duang Thai two-stringed bowed lute with wooden body

Saw sam sai Three-string bowed lute and the leader of the Thai mahori ensemble

Saw u Thai two stringed bowed lute with coconut shell body

Shin byu Monk initiation ceremony in Burma

Sralai Khmer reed aerophone

Stupa A shrine containing a real or symbolic relic of the Buddha (see pagoda)

Sutta/Suttra Scriptures of Buddhist canonical texts

Syllabic Singing with one syllable of text per note

Tai A variety of ethnic groups speaking related tonal languages (Tai-Kada)

Tân nhạc Vietnamese modern popular fusion music with Western instrumentation and orchestration

Thachin Songs (Burmese)

Thachin' Gyi Great Songs. The cannon or court music in Burma/ Myanmar

Tayaw Ancient Burmese bowed lute. Contemporary term for violin

Theravada Buddhism "The way of the elders," branch of Buddhism found in Sri Lanka, Burma/Myanmar, Thailand, and Cambodia

Thon Thai goblet-shaped drum

Timbre Particular quality of sound; tone color

Tripitaka Literally "the three baskets," the Buddhist Pali canon. The tripitika consists of the vinaya pitaka (Buddhist law or code of conduct), the sutta pitaka (accounts of the Buddha's teaching), and the Abhidhamma pitaka (commentaries on Buddhist teaching and law).

Việt The dominant ethnic group of Vietnam (see Kinh)

Vinaya Buddhist law

Wa let kouke Large bamboo clapper

Wai khru Ritual initiation of students and honoring of teachers in the Thai tradition

Wat Literally "school." A Buddhist temple or monastery in Cambodia, Thailand or Laos

Yodaya Burmese word for Thailand and a genre of Thai-influnced songs in the Burmese court repertoire.

Yamayana Burmese version of the Hindu Ramayana

References

Arana, Miranda. 1999. *Neotraditional Music in Vietnam*. Special Volume of Nhạc Việt *The Journal of Vietnamese Music*. Kent, Ohio: Nhạc Việt.

Aung Zaw. 2004. "Burma: Music Under Seige." In Marie Korpe ed. *Shoot the Singer! Music Censorship Today*. New York: Zed Books, 39–61.

Allott, Anna J. 1993. *Inked Over, Ripped Out: Burmese Storytellers and the Censors*. Chiang Mai: Silkworm Books.

Aung Zaw, ed. 2002. "Sound Effects: Politics and Popular Music in Burma." In *The Irrawaddy*. Vol. 10 No. 7. Chiang Mai, Thailand, www.irrawaddy.org.

Barmé, Scot. 1993. *Luang Wichit Wathakan and the Creation of a Thai Identity*. Singapore: ISEAS.

Becker, Judith. 1967. "The Migration of the Arched Harp from India to Burma." *Galpin Society Journal* xx: 17–23.

——. 1968. "Percussive Patterns in the Music of Mainland Southeast Asia." *Ethnomusicology* 12(2): 173–191.

Catlin, Amy. 1981. *Music of the Hmong: Singing Voices and Talking Reeds*. Providence, R.I.: Center for Hmong Lore.

——. 1997. *Hmong musicians in America: Interactions with Three Generations of Hmong Americans 1978–1996* [videorecording] [produced and directed] by Amy Catlin and Nazir Jairazbhoy; written, edited, and narrated by Amy Catlin. Van Nuys, CA: Apsara Media for Intercultural Education. c.1997.

Central Intelligence Agency. 2008. "The 2008 World Factbook." https://www.cia.gov/library/publications/the-world-factbook/ (accessed May 2008).

Chaterjee, Partha. 1993. *The Nation and its Fragments*. Princeton NJ: Princeton University Press.

Compton, Carol. 1992. "Traditional Verbal Arts in Laos: Functions, Forms, Continuities, and Changes in Texts, Contexts, and Performances." *Selected Reports in Ethnomusicology* 9:149–159.

Cox, Sherry Lee. 1986. "A Burmese Classical Song: Text-Music Relationships in the you:daya: song Mya Man: Gi-ri." M.A. thesis, University of Hawaii.

Douglas, Gavin. 2005. "Burmese Music and the World Market." *Anthropology Today*. Vol. 21. Issue 6, December: 5–9.

Douglas, Gavin. 2005. "Myanmar (Burma)." In *Encyclopedia of Popular Music of the World*, Vol. 4, ed. John Shepherd, David Horn, Dave Laing, Paul Oliver and Peter Wicke. London: Continuum International Publishing Group, 196–202.

——. 2003. "The Myanmar University of Culture: For Patriotism and National Unity." *Journal of Chinese Ritual, Theatre and Folklore*. Vol. 141 (September): 261–281.

——. 2003. "The Sokayeti Performing Arts Competition of Burma/ Myanmar." *The World of Music*. Vol. 45 (1): 35–54.

Duriyanga, Phra Chen. 1990a. *Thai Music. Thai Culture*, New Series No. 15. Bangkok: The Promotion and Public Relations Sub-Division, The Fine Arts Department (first published 1948).

——. 1990b. *Thai Music in Western Notation*. Thai Culture, New Series No. 16. Bangkok: The Promotion and Public Relations Sub-Division, The Fine Arts Department (first published 1951).

Duy, Pham. 1975. *Musics of Vietnam*. Carbondale and Edwardsville: Southern Illinois University Press.

Falk, Catherine. 2003/2004. "The Dragon Taught Us: Hmong Stories about the Origin of the Free Reed Pipes, Qeej." *Journal of Asian Music* 35 (1), 2003/2004: 17–56.

——. 2003. " 'If you have good knowledge, close it well tight': Concealed and framed meaning in the funeral music of the Hmong qeej." *British Journal of Ethnomusicology* 12 (ii): 1–33.

——. 2004. "The private and public lives of the Hmong qeej or Miao lusheng." In *Changing Cultural Contexts: Representations of the Hmong*, ed. Nicholas Tapp. Canberra, ACT: Pandanus Press.

Garfias, Robert. 1975a. "A Musical Visit to Burma." *The World of Music* 18 (1): 3–13.

——. 1975b. "Preliminary Thoughts on Burmese Modes." *Asian Music* 7(1): 39–49.

——. 1985. "The Development of the Modern Burmese Hsaing Ensemble." *Asian Music* 16:1–28.

Garofalo, Reebee. 2007. "Pop goes to war, 2001–2004: U.S. Popular Music After 9/11." In *Music in the Post-9/11 World*, ed. Jonathan Ritter and Martin Daughtry. New York: Routledge.

Gibbs, Jason. 2003/2004. "The West's Songs, Our Songs: The Introduction and Adaptation of Western Popular Song in Vietnam before 1940." *Asian Music* 35(1): 57–83.

——. 2000. "Spoken Theater, La Scene Tonkinoise, and the First Modern Vietnamese Songs." *Asian Music* 31(2) (Spring-Summer 2000):1–33.

——. 1988. "Nhac Tien Chien: The Origins of Vietnamese Popular Song." *Destination Vietnam* online, June/July 1998, (accessed August 29, 2008).

Greene, Paul and Li Wei. 2004. "Introduction: Mindfulness and Change in Buddhist Musical Traditions." *Asian Music* 35(2):1–6.

Greene, Paul. 2004. "The Dhamma as Sonic Praxis: Paritta Chant in Burmese Theravada Buddhism." *Asian Music* 35(2): 43–78.

———. 2002. "Buddhism and the Musical Cultures of Asia: An Annotated Discography." With Kieth Howard, Terry E. Miller, Steven G. Nelson, Phong T. Nguyen, and Hwee-San Tan. *Asian Music* 35(2): 133–74.

———. 2002. "Buddhism and the Musical Cultures of Asia: A Critical Literature Survey." With Keith Howard, Terry Miller, Phong Nguyen, and Hwee-San Tan. *The World of Music* 44(2):135–75.

Gronow, Pekka. 1981. "The Record Industry Comes to the Orient." *Ethnomusicology* 25(2): 251–284.

Hla Pe. 1985. "The Shin-byú-bwè in Burma." In *Burma: Literature, Historiography, Scholarship, Language, Life, and Buddhism,* Singapore: Institute of Southeast Asian Studies: 178–85.

Irrawaddy River. [Map/Still]. Retrieved August 10, 2009, from Britannica Student Encyclopedia: http://student.britannica.com/ebi/art-556.

Jirattikorn, Amporn. 2006. "*Lukthung*: Authenticity and Modernity in Thai Country Music." *Asian Music* (Winter/Spring): 24–50.

Keeler, Ward. 2009. "What's Burmese About Burmese Rap?: Why Some Expressive Forms Go Global." *American Ethnologist* 36(1): 2–19.

———. 1998. "Burma." In *The Garland Encyclopedia of World Music, Southeast Asia.* Vol. 4. ed. Terry E. Miller and Sean Williams. New York: Garland Publishing.

Keyes, Charles. 1995. *The Golden Peninsula: Culture and Adaptation in Mainland Southeast Asia.* 2nd ed. Honolulu: University of Hawaii Press.

———. 2002. "Science and Politics in the Classification of Ethnic Groups in Thailand, China, and Vietnam." *The Journal of Asian Studies* 61(4): 1163–1203.

Keyes, Charles and Shigeharu Tanabe, eds. 2002. *Cultural Crisis and Social Memory: Modernity and Identity in Thailand and Laos.* London: Routledge Curzon.

Khin Yi. 1988. *The Dobama Movement in Burma (1930–1938).* New York: Southeast Asia Program Cornell University.

Khin Zaw, U. 1940a. "Burmese Music: A Preliminary Enquiry." *Journal of the Burma Research Society* XXX, Part III (December): 387–466.

———. 1940b. "Burmese Music (A Preliminary Enquiry)." *Bulletin of the School of Oriental and African Studies* 10 (3): 717–754.

———. 1956. "Burmese Culture." *Orient Review and Literary Digest* 2: 5–17.

———. 1958. "Burmese Music: A Partnership in Melodic Patterns." *The Atlantic Monthly* 201: 163–165.

———. 1961. "Burmese Music." *Open Mind* 2 (12): 175–214.

Ko Shoon Myaing. 2001. *International Notation and Myanmar Classical Songs.* Mandalay Myoma Amateur Music Association.

Lau, Frederick. 2008. *Music in China: Experiencing Music, Expressing Culture.* New York: Oxford University Press.

Leach, Edmund Ronald. 1977 (1954). *Political Systems of Highland Burma: A Study of Kachin Social Structure.* London: Athlone Press.

Lintner, Bertil. 1989. "Politics of Pop." *Far Eastern Economic Review* (22 June): 40.

Mabbett, Ian W. 1993–94. "Buddhism and Music." *Asian Music* 25(1/2): 9–28.

Mackerras, Colin 1987. "Theater in Vietnam." *Asian Theatre Journal.* Vol. 4. No. 1. (Spring 1987): 1–28.

Madison, Olivia. 2005. "Cambodia: Of Sounds and Survival – Khmer music." *Freemuse: Freedom of Musical Expression,* www.freemuse.com (accessed November 27, 2008).

Mahindarama Buddhist Temple. 2002. *Vandanā: The Album of Pāḷi Devotional Chanting & Hymns.* Malaysia: Mahindarama Dhamma Publication.

Marcus, Scott. 2007. *Music in Egypt: Experiencing Music, Expressing Culture.* New York: Oxford University Press.

McNamer, M. 1986. "Musical Change and Change in Music: Implications for Hmong Identity." In *The Hmong World,* ed. Brenda Johns and David Strecker. New Haven, CT: Council on Southeast Asia Studies: 137–163.

Miller, Terry E. 1983. "To The Editor." *Asian Music* 14(2): 190.

——. 1985. *Traditional Music of the Laos: Khaen Playing and Mawlum Singing in North-East Thailand.* Greenwood Press 1985.

——. 1991. *An Introduction to Playing the Kaen.* Kent, OH: World Music Enterprises.

——. 1998. "Thailand." In *The Garland Encyclopedia of World Music: Southeast Asia,* ed. Terry Miller and Sean Williams. New York and London: Garland Publishing, 218–334.

——. 1998. "Laos." In *The Garland Encyclopedia of World Music: Southeast Asia,* ed. Terry Miller and Sean Williams. New York and London: Garland Publishing, 335–362.

——. 1992. "The Theory and Practice of Thai Musical Notations." *Ethnomusicology* 36(2) (Spring- Summer 1992): 197–221.

——. 2005. "From Country Hick to Rural Hip: A New Identity through Music for Northeast Thailand." *Asian Music.* Vol. 36, No. 2. (Summer/ Fall 2005): 96–106.

Miller, Terry E. and Sam-Ang Sam. 1995. "The Classical Musics of Cambodia and Thailand: A Study of Distinctions." *Ethnomusicology* 39(2): 229–243.

Miller, Terry and Sean Williams. 2008. "Waves of Cultural Influence." In *The Garland Handbook of Southeast Asian Music,* ed. Terry E. Miller and Sean Williams. New York: Routledge, 28–56.

———. 2008. "The Impact of Modernization on Traditional Musics." In *The Garland Handbook of Southeast Asian Music*, ed. Terry E. Miller and Sean Williams. New York: Routledge, 65–79.

Min Zin. 2003. "Ethnic Entertainers Make the Scene." *The Irrawaddy*. May 2003: 30–31.

Morrison, Gayle. 1998. "The Hmong Qeej: Speaking to the Spirit World." *Hmong Studies Journal* 2(2) (Spring 1998) http://www.hmongstudies. org/HmongStudiesJournal (accessed July 26, 2008).

Moua, B.X. 1996. *Boua Xou Moua. The Music of the Hmong People of Laos.* (CD liner notes). Dallas, Tx: Documentary Arts Inc. Arhoolie CD 446.

Myers-Moro, Pamela. 1993. *Thai Music and Musicians in Contemporary Bangkok.* Berkeley: Centers for South and Southeast Asia Studies, University of California at Berkeley.

———. 1990. "Musical Notation in Thailand." *Journal of the Siam Society* 78: 101–108.

Morgan, Susan. 2008. *Bombay Anna: The Real Story and Remarkable Adventures of the King and I Governess.* Berkeley: University of California Press.

Moro, Pamela. 2004. "Constructions of Nation and the Classicization of the Music: Comparative Perspectives from Southeast and South Asia." *Journal of Southeast Asian Studies* 35 (2): 187–211.

Nguyen, Phong T. 2008. "Vietnam." In *The Garland Handbook of Southeast Asian Music*, ed. Terry E. Miller and Sean Williams. New York: Routledge, 247–290.

———. 2003. "Vietnamese Music in America." *Institute for Vietnamese Music.* http://www.vietnamesemusic.us/NTP1.html (accessed June 2008).

———. 2002. "Music and Movement in Vietnamese Buddhism." *The World of Music* 44(2): 57–71.

———. 1998. "Minority Musics of Vietnam." In *The Garland Encyclopedia of World Music: Southeast Asia*, ed. Terry Miller and Sean Williams. New York and London: Garland Publishing, 531–536.

———. 1995. "Vietnam." In *The Garland Encyclopedia of World Music Southeast Asia*, ed. Terry Miller and Sean Williams. New York and London: Garland Publishing, 444–517.

———. 1992. "Text, Context and Performance: A Case Study of the Vietnamese Buddhist Liturgy." In *Text, Context, and Performance in Cambodia, Laos and Vietnam*, ed. Amy Catlin. Los Angeles: University of California, Los Angeles, Dept. of Ethnomusicology, 225–32.

Norodom, Buppha Devi. 2000. *Reports on Work Activities in the Domain of Cultural and Fine Arts in Year 2000 and the Goals of year 2001.* Phnom Penh: Department of Study, Research, and Work Balance, Ministry of Culture and Fine Arts.

Nu Nu Yi. 2008. *Smile As They Bow.* New York: Hyperion.

Olsen, Dale A. 2008. *Popular Music of Vietnam: The Politics of Remembering the Economics of Forgetting*. New York: Routledge.

Pham Duy. 1975. *Musics of Vietnam*. Ed. Dale R. Whiteside. Carbondale and Edwardsville: Southern Illinois University Press.

Picken, L.E.R. 1984. "Making of the Khaen: The Free-Reed Mouth Organ of North-East Thailand." *Musica Asiatica* 14: 117–154.

Reid, Anthony. 1995. *Southeast Asia in the Age of Commerce, 1450–1680*, Vol. 2 of *Expansion and Crisis*. New Haven: Yale University Press.

Renan, Ernest. 1996. "What is a Nation?" *Becoming National: A Reader*. New York and Oxford: Oxford University Press, 41–55.

Reyes-Schramm, Adelaida. 1999. *Songs of the Caged, Songs of the Free: Music and the Vietnamese Refugee Experience*. Philadelphia: Temple University Press.

Sam, Sam-Ang, Panya Roongrüang, and Phong T. Nguyen. 1995. "The Khmer People." In *The Garland Encyclopedia of World Music: Southeast Asia*, ed. Terry Miller and Sean Williams. New York and London: Garland Publishing, 151–217.

Sam, Sam Ang. 2003. "Cultural Policies of Cambodia." *Journal of Chinese Ritual, Theatre and Folklore*. Vol. 141, September 2003: 213–236.

——. 2007. "Transmission of Khmer Traditional Performing Arts: Its Genuineness, Challenge, and Impact on Society." In *Authenticity and Cultural Identity: Performing Arts in Southeast Asia*, ed. Yoshitaka Terada. Osaka, Japan: National Museum of Ethnology, Senri Ethnological Reports 65, 123–136.

Schafer, John C. 2007. "The Trinh Cong Son Phenomenon." *The Journal of Asian Studies* 66(3): 597–643.

Schlund-Vials, Cathy J. 2008. "A Transnational Hip Hop Nation: praCh, Cambodia, and Memorialising the Killing Fields." *Life Writing*. Vol. 5, Issue 1 April 2008: 11–27.

Scott, James C. 1998. *Seeing Like a State: How Certain Schemes to Improve the Human Condition Have Failed*. The Yale ISPS Series. New Haven and London: Yale University Press.

Sein, Kenneth (Maung Khe), and J.A. Withey. 1965. *The Great Po Sein: A Chronicle of Burmese Theatre*. Bloomington and London: Indiana University Press.

Shapiro-Phim, Toni. 2002. "Dance, Music and the Nature of Terror in Democratic Kampuchea." In *Annihilating Difference: The Anthropology of Genocide*, ed. Alexander Laban Hinton. Berkeley: University of California Press, 179–193.

Simonson, Linda. 1987. "A Burmese Arched Harp (Saùng-gauk) and Its Pervasive Buddhist Symbolism." *Journal of the American Musical Instrument Society* 13: 39–64.

Siriyuvasak, Ubonrat. 1990. "Commercializing the Sound of the People: Pleng Luktoong and the Thai Pop Music Industry." *Popular Music* 9(1):61–77.

Smith, Martin. 1991. "State of Fear: Censorship in Burma (Myanmar)." *An Article 19 Country Report*. London: Article 19.

South, Ashley. 2007. "Karen Nationalist Communities: The 'Problem' of Diversity." *Contemporary Southeast Asia* 29(1): 55–76.

Spiro, Melford. 1996. *Burmese Supernaturalism: A Study in the Explanation and Reduction of Suffering*. Exp. ed. New Jersey: Prentice Hall Inc. (first published 1967).

Steger, Manfred B. 2003. *Globalization: A Very Short Introduction*. New York: Oxford University Press.

Stokes, Martin. 2004. "Music and the Global Order." *Annual Review Anthropology* 33: 47–72.

Tan, Amy. 2005. *Saving Fish From Drowning*. New York: Random House.

Tambiah, Stanley J. 1970. *Buddhism and the Spirit Cults in North-East Thailand*. Cambridge: Cambridge University Press, 1970.

Tarling, Nicholas. 2001. *Southeast Asia: A Modern History*. New York: Oxford University Press.

Thao, Yer J. 2006. "Culture and Knowledge of the Sacred Instrument Qeej in the Mong-American Community." *Asian Folklore Studies* 65: 249–267.

Thao, H. 1995. *Hmong Music in Vietnam*. Special Issue of *Nhac Viet, the Journal of Vietnamese Music* 4(2), Fall 1995.

Uchida, Ruriko and Amy Catlin. 1998. "Music of Upland Minorities in Burma, Laos, and Thailand." In *The Garland Encyclopedia of World Music: Southeast Asia*, ed. Terry Miller and Sean Williams. New York and London: Garland Publishing, 537–559.

Wade, Bonnie. 2009. *Thinking Musically: Experiencing Music, Expressing Culture*. 2nd ed. New York: Oxford.

Williams, Sean. 2006. "Buddhism and Music." In *Sacred Sound: Experiencing Music in World Religions*, ed. Guy L. Beck. Waterloo: Wilfrid Laurier University Press, 169–189.

Williamson, Muriel C. 1968. "The Construction and Decoration of One Burmese Harp," *Selected Reports in Ethnomusicology* 1 (2): 45–72.

———. 1979. "A biographical note on Myá-wadi U Sá, Burmese poet and composer." In *Musica Asiatica 2*. London: Oxford University Press, 151–154.

Womack, William. 2005. "Literate Networks and the Production of Sgaw and Pwo Karen Writing in Burma, c.1830–1930". Ph.D. dissertation, School of African and Oriental Studies, University of London.

Wong, Deborah. 2004. *Speak it Louder: Asian Americans Making Music*. New York: Routledge.

Wong, Deborah. 2003. "Plugged in at Home: Vietnamese American Technoculture in Orange County." In *Music and Technoculture*, ed. René T. A. Lysloff and Leslie Gay. Hanover, NH: Wesleyan University Press, 125–152.

———. 2001. *Sounding the Center: History and Aesthetics in Thai Buddhist Performance.* Chicago: University of Chicago Press.

———. 1998. "Mon Music for Thai Deaths: Ethnicity and Status in Thai Urban Funerals." *Asian Folklore Studies* 57(1): 99–130.

———. 1989/90. "Thai Cassettes and Their Covers: Two Case Histories." *Asian Music* 21(1):78–104.

Wong, Deborah and Rene Lysloff. 1991. "Threshold to the Sacred: The Overture in Thai and Javanese Ritual Performance." *Ethnomusicology* 35(3): 315–348.

Wright, Arnold, ed. 1910. "Misquith & Co." In *Twentieth Century Impressions of Burma: Its History, People, Commerce, Industries and Resources.* London: Lloyd's Greater Britain Publishing Company, 351.

Wyatt, David K. 1969. *Thailand: A Short History.* 2nd ed. New Haven: Yale University Press.

Additional Resources

Reading

Catlin, Amy. ed. 1992. "Text, Context, and Performance in Cambo, Laos and Vietnam." In *Selected Reports in Ethnomusicology.* Vol. X. Los Angeles: University of California.

Catlin, Amy. 1992. *Khmer Classical Dance Songbook.* Van Nuys, California: Apsara Media for Intercultural Education.

Charney, Michael W. 2009. *A History of Modern Burma.* Cambridge: Cambridge University Press.

Cravath, Paul. 1986. "The Ritual Origins of the Classical Dance Drama of Cambodia." *Asian Theater Journal* 3(2): 179–203.

Lafreniere, Bree. 2000. *Music Through the Dark: A Tale of Survival in Cambodia.* Honolulu: University of Hawaii Press.

Lockard, Craig A. 1998. *Dance of Life: Popular Music and Politics in Southeast Asia.* Chiang Mai: Silkworm Books.

Miller, Terry and Jarernchai Chonpairot. 1994. *A History of Siamese Music Reconstructed from Western Documents, 1505–1932.* Special issue of *Crossroads: An Interdisciplinary Journal of Southeast Asian Studies.* Center for Southeast Asian Studies, Northern Illinois University.

Miller, Terry and Sean Williams (eds). 1998. *The Garland Encyclopedia of World Music: Southeast Asia.* New York and London: Garland Publishing.

Morton, David. 1976. *The Traditional Music of Thailand.* Berkeley: University of California Press.

Nguyen, Phong. 2003. "Vietnamese Music after the Revolution: Reevaluation and Modernization." In *Cultural Policy and Traditional Performing Arts in Asia, Journal of Chinese Ritual, Theatre and Folklore.* Vol. 141, September.

Nguyen, Phong Thuyet, and Patricia Shehan Campbell. 1990. *From Rice Paddies and Temple Yards: Traditional Music of Vietnam,* Danbury, CT: World Music Press.

MacLaughlan, Heather. 2006. "The Don Dance: An Expression of Karen Nationalism." In *VOICES: The Journal of New York Folklore* 32(3–4): 26–32.

McGraw, Andrew. 2007. "The *Pia*'s Subtle Sustain: Contemporary ethnic Identity and the Revitalization of the *Lanna* 'Heart Harp.'" *Asian Music* 38(2): 115–142.

Myers-Moro, Pamela. 1986. "'Songs for life': Leftist Thai popular music in the 1970s." *Journal of Popular Culture* 20(3): 93–113.

Perris, Arnold. 1995. *Music as Propaganda: Art to Persuade, Art to Control.* Vol. 8. Westport, CT: Greenwood Press.

Phoasavadi, Pornprapit "Ros" and Patricia Shehan Campbell. 2003. *From Bangkok and Beyond: Thai Children's Songs, Games and Customs*, Danbury, CT: World Music Press.

Reyes-Schramm, Adelida. 1986. "Tradition in the Guise of Innovation: Music among a Refugee Population." *ICTM Yearbook*: 91–101.

SarDesai, D. R. ed. *Southeast Asian History: Essential Readings.* Westview Press.

Sam, Sam-Ang. 1988. The Pin Peat Ensemble: Its History, Music and Context. PhD diss., Wesleyan University.

Sam, Sam-Ang and Patricia Shehan Campbell. 1992. *"Silent Temples, Songful Hearts: Traditional Music of Cambodia."* Danbury, CT: World Music Press.

Shahriari, Andrew. 2006. *Khon Muang Music and Dance Traditions of North Thailand.* Bangkok, Thailand: White Lotus Press.

Swangviboonpong, Dusadee. 2003. *Thai Classical Singing: Its History, Musical Characteristics, and Transmission.* Aldershot, Hampshire: Ashgate, 2003.

Swearer, Donald K. 1995. *The Buddhist World of Southeast Asia.* Albany: State University of New York Press.

Terada, Yoshitaka. 2007. *Authenticity and Cultural Identity: Performing Arts in Southeast Asia.* National Museum of Ethnology, Senri Ethnological Reports 65.

Tran, Van Khe. 1968. "Musique bouddhique au Vietnam." In Jacques Porte et al., eds., *Encyclopédie des musiques sacrées.* Vol. 1. Paris: Edition Labergerie: 222–40.

Tran, Van Khe. 1975. "Vietnamese Music." *Selected Reports in Ethnomusicology* 2:35–47.

Listening

Boua Xou Moua. *The Music of the Hmong People of Laos.* (Music CD). Dallas, Tx: Documentary Arts Inc., 1996.

Fong Nam: Ancient Contemporary Music from Thailand Tucson, AZ: Celestial Harmonies, 1995.

Green Tea Leaf Salad: Flavors of Burmese Music. 2000. Various Artists. PAN Records. Rick Heizman, Producer. PAN 2083.

Hsaing Waing of Myanmar. cp1992. Various Artists. World Music Library, King Records: Tokyo, Japan. KICC 5162.

Isan Slete/The Flower of Isan. Globestyle CD OR BD051. 1989.

The Jazz King: H.M. The King Bhumibol Musical Composition The Jazz King: H.M. The King Bhumibol Musical Composition. Performed by Larry Carlton & Guests.

Karenni: Music from the border areas of Thailand and Burma. Various Artists. cp1994 Paradox. The Netherlands: Pan Records. Liner notes by Fred Gales. Pan 2040CD.

Khamvong Insixiengmai: Bamboo voices: folk music from Laos. Khamvong Insixiengmai ensemble. Chapel Hill, NC: Owl's Head Music, 1996.

Ko Ko, U. *Piano birman/Burmese piano.* cp1995. Produced by Lorraine Chalifoux. UMMUS UMM 203. (Série traditions.) (1 CD). Notes (11p.) in French and English by Robert Garfias. Performer: U Ko Ko/ piano. Co-production of University of Montreal and the Société Radio-Canada.

Mahagitá: Harp and Vocal Music of Burma. 2003. U Myint Maung and Daw Yi Yi Thant. Smithsonian Folkways Recordings. SFW CD 40492.

Mo lam singing of Northeast Thailand. Tokyo, Japan: King Records, 1991.

Mother Mountain and Father Sea. Dr. Phong T. Nguyen and Dr. Terry E. Miller, producers. Incline Village, NV: White Cliffs Media, 2003 (6 CDs).

Music of Myanmar. cp1988. Various Artists World Music Library, King Records: Tokyo, Japan. KICC 5132.

Music of Northeast Thailand. Various Artists. World Music Library KICC 5159, 1992.

Music of Northeast Thailand. Tokyo, Japan: King Record Co., 1992.

The Music of Vietnam 3 CD Boxed Set [BOX SET], Celestial Harmonies.

Musicians of the National Dance Company of Cambodia. Homrong Musicians of the National Dance Company of Cambodia. Beverly Hills, CA: Real World Records/Virgin Records, 1991.

Royal Court Music of Thailand. Washington, D.C.: Smithsonian Folkways, 1994.

Sam, Sam-Ang. *Sam-Ang Sam Ensemble. Mohori: Khmer music from Cambodia* Sam-Ang Sam Ensemble. Chapel Hill, NC: Music of the World, 1997.

—— *Sam-Ang Sam Ensemble.: Echoes from the palace* Chapel Hill, N.C.: Music of the World, 1996.

Sandaya U Yee Nwe. *Sandaya: The Spellbinding Piano of Burma. Featuring: U Yee Nwe.* cp1988. Produced by Rick Heizman. Shanachie 66007 (1 CD). Recorded in Rangoon, Burma.

Sein Kyaw Kyaw Naing. *Pat Waing: The Magic Drum Circle of Burma. Featuring: Kyaw Kyaw Naing.* cp1988. Produced by Rick Heizman. Shanachie 66005 (1 CD). Recorded in Rangoon, Burma.

Song of the Banyan: Folk Music of Vietnam. 1997. Phong Nguyen Ensemble. Latitudes. LAT 50607.

Song of the Banyan. Phong Nguyen Ensemble. Chapel Hill, NC: Latitudes, 1997.

String Instruments of Vietnam. Tokyo, Japan: King Records, 1991.

Thai Elephant Orchestra Dave Soldier, Richard Lair. [Lampang, Thailand]: Mulatta Records, c2000.

Thailande: La musique des Mons: France: Playa Sound; Paris: Distribution, Auvidis, 1988, c1976.

Vietnamese Traditional Music by Pham Duch Thanh. 2005. Pham Duc Thanh and Vieu Nguyet Lan. Oliver Sudden Productions, Inc (1 CD).

White Elephants and Golden Ducks: Enchanting Musical Treasures from Burma. cp1997. Musicians: Kyaw Kyaw Naing, U Tin Yi, U Yee Nwe, Daw Yi Yi Thant, U Zaw Win Maung. Produced by Rick Heizman. Shanachie 64087. (1 CD). Recorded in Rangoon, Burma.

Viewing

Catlin, Amy. 1997. *Hmong musicians in America: Interactions with Three Generations of Hmong Americans 1978–1996* [videorecording] [produced and directed] by Amy Catlin and Nazir Jairazbhoy; written, edited, and narrated by Amy Catlin. Van Nuys, CA: Apsara Media for Intercultural Education, c1997.

—— 1991. *From Angkor to America: The Cambodian Dance and Music Project of Van Nuys, California, 1984–1990,* Apsara Media for Intercultural Education.

Glatzer, Jocelyn. 2003. *The Flute Player.* Distributed by NAATA Distribution National Asian American Telecommunications Association www.naata-net.org.shopnaata

Ingleton, Sally. 1993. *The Tenth Dancer.* Distributed by Women Making Movies, www.wmm.com

JVC Video Anthology of World Music and Dance: Southeast Asia I, Vol. 6, *Southeast Asia II,* Vol. 7, Ichikawa Katsumori Producer.

Kersalé, Patrick. 2003. *Vietnam/Hmong: The Art of Attraction* 2003. Patrick Kersale, World Music Discoveries, Playa Sound Horizons. Sunset France, www.playsound.com

Marre, Jeremy. 1983/1994. *Two Faces of Thailand: A Musical Portrait.* Beats of the Heart, Shanachie Video.

Ostergaard, Anders. 2008. *Burma VJ,* International Documentary Feature Films. Denmark, 85 mins., color.

The Overture directed by Itthi-sunthorn Wichailak. Distributed by Kino International. Thai with English Subtitles.

Poss, Nicholas. 2001. *Speaking Musically: An Introduction to Traditional Hmong Music.* Open Source Movies, http://www.archive.org/details/Nicholas PossSpeakingMusicallyAnIntroductiontoTraditionalHmongMusic

Index

∞